To Duncan on

Happy

W

C000150242

1.

SWALEDALE

'Beautiful Swaledale, the land of rest,
Beautiful Swaledale, I love thee the best.
The land is set in a cultivate style;
The extension of Swaledale is twenty long mile.'
                                          Yorkshire ballad

SWALEDALE

A David Leather

Smith
Settle

First published in 1992 by
Smith Settle Ltd
Ilkley Road
Otley
West Yorkshire
LS21 3JP

ISBN 1 870071 91 3

British Library Cataloguing-in-Publication Data:
A catalogue record for this book is available
from the British Library.

Designed, printed and bound by
SMITH SETTLE
Ilkley Road, Otley, West Yorkshire LS21 3JP

CONTENTS

For Brian, who will have a go

INTRODUCTION

This volume is one of a new series called *Walker's Guides* and explores the wild and remote area of Swaledale from the attractive little town of Richmond to the top of Nine Standards Rigg at the head of the dale.

Swaledale is a walker's delight. Once the hub of a valuable leadmining industry, the area is now criss-crossed with footpaths which were formerly packhorse routes to and from the mines and smelt mills, and tracks which miners used daily from village to mine. In places there are so many rights of way that maps show a veritable maze of enticing footpaths and bridleways. There are also old drove roads, now the walled green lanes of the Dales, and unclassified county highways that are no more than tracks. Most walkers are to be seen on the long-distance Coast-to-Coast path which follows the north side of Swaledale, and the Pennine Way which crosses from north to south. This leaves 250 miles (400km) of quiet, unfrequented ways just waiting to be tramped.

The guide not only gives you directions for a carefully-chosen selection of twenty of the best walks, but fills you in on details of historical events, personalities, stories and folk tales. It draws attention to the wildlife and flora you are likely to see on each walk, together with an explanation of the scenery and mining history. The circular walks vary from 3½ to 10½ miles (5½–17km), so there should be plenty of time to look at the world about you. Add a third to the time stated at the beginning of each walk to allow for picnics or taking photographs.

For each walk, the route and nearby features are shown on a clear map and, together with the directions, should be sufficient to find the way. If you like to have an Ordnance Survey map with you, the best is the 1:25,000 Outdoor Leisure Map 30 (2½ inches to the mile), *The Yorkshire Dales, Northern and Central Areas.* You get double the value from this map because it has Swaledale on one side, and Wensleydale and upper Wharfedale on the other. The two extremities of the dale need additional Pathfinder maps, numbers 608 and 609. In using grid references, given at the beginning of each walk, read along the foot (or top) of the map first, then up the side.

The beautifully-executed line drawings and watercolours of birds and flowers are by Philip Bartlett, with some fine colour photographs by John Edenbrow and Trevor Croucher. Maps, diagrams and other photographs are by the author. Quotation of grid references is by courtesy of the Ordnance Survey.

I would like to thank David Perray for his enthusiastic help on the birds and mammals of Swaledale, Tony Wood who gave valuable advice about the flora, Roger Smith for information about hay meadows, David Morris on aspects of history and Laurence Barker on information about Calver Hill; thanks, too, to Sue Arnott of the Yorkshire Dales National Park for imparting her intimate knowledge of access and rights of way, and to the helpful and friendly staff of Richmond Public Library. A final thank you goes to Mark Whitley and Smith Settle for their help and encouragement, and for the successful design of the series.

When you are out in the Dales, take back with you happy memories, notes, sketches or photographs but please leave undisturbed the wild flowers, rocks and fossils for the enjoyment of other walkers. Respect the people who live and work in the countryside and remember the Country Code.

A D Leather
Ilkley, 1992

ACKNOWLEDGMENTS

Thanks are due to the following people for permission to reproduce the undermentioned illustrations:

Phillip Bartlett: p19, 20, 22, 23, 26, 27, 29, 30, 31, 32, 40, 41, 46, 51(*l*), 63, 71, 77, 81, 99, 102,
Trevor Croucher: front cover, p4, 5, 8, 103, 106, 111,
John Edenbrow: p34, 59, 118

All other illustrations were provided by the author.

There is no rail link to Swaledale, the nearest stations to Richmond being at Northallerton and Darlington. There is a daily bus service from Darlington to Richmond. At weekends in the summer there are occasional buses to Keld from Leeds, Harrogate and Bradford.

On Tuesdays and Saturdays there is a morning bus from Richmond to the Tan Hill road end just beyond Keld which calls at Reeth, Gunnerside and the villages along the dale. The return bus is early in the afternoon with a later bus from Gunnerside only. The bus service is useful for walks from the villages *en route* or for a linear walk along the riverside or the Coast-to-Coast path.

Check the timetables carefully and make use of the comprehensive timetable entitled *Dales Connections*, free from the tourist information centres in Richmond and Reeth or from United Automobile Services Ltd, Grange Road, Darlington, Co Durham (phone 0325 468771), in which all the Dales bus services are given.

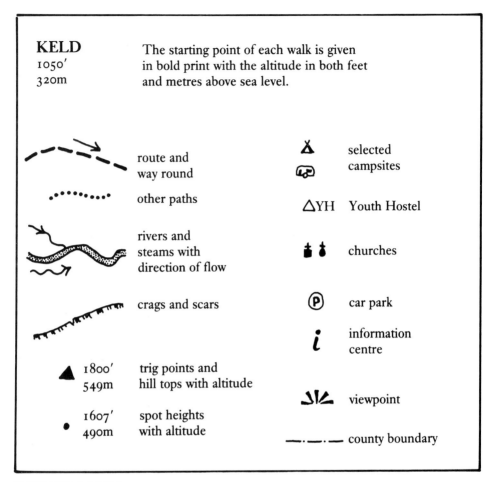

KELD
1050′
320m

The starting point of each walk is given in bold print with the altitude in both feet and metres above sea level.

route and way round

other paths

rivers and steams with direction of flow

crags and scars

▲ 1800′ 549m trig points and hill tops with altitude

● 1607′ 490m spot heights with altitude

selected campsites

△YH Youth Hostel

churches

Ⓟ car park

i information centre

viewpoint

—.—.— county boundary

KEY TO MAPS

Overall Map

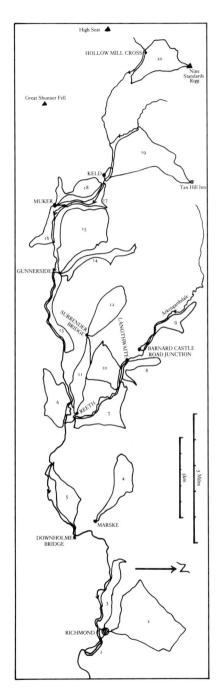

ROCKS AND THE LANDSCAPE

For many people, Swaledale is the loveliest and most magical of the Yorkshire Dales, its wild beauty and romanticism being particularly appealing. The landscape combines all that is best in the Dales, and the views from Kisdon or Crackpot, from above Ivelet or Fremington Edge, are as scenic as any picture postcard. Narrower and more winding than Wensleydale, its steeply sloping sides are closer together, giving it an intimacy that other dales lack, and its sinuous valley provides ever-changing aspects as the visitor travels between Richmond and Keld. But, being just that much further from the cities and towns, the dale sees fewer tourists and tends to be more peaceful, old-fashioned and unchanging with time.

The headstreams of the Swale rise way up on the slopes of High Seat and Nine Standards Rigg on the main watershed of England and, where the becks of Birkdale and Great Sleddale meet, there begins the real Swale as it descends rapidly towards Keld. The river plunges first over Wain Wath Force and then into a narrow gorge below the village and over the almost hidden Catrake Force, followed by the lovely falls of Kisdon Force.

As it swings along its partly-wooded valley, it descends another 650 feet (200m) along the next 20 miles (48km) to Richmond Bridge, a fall of 35 feet per mile (6.5m/km). As a result, the Swale is a remarkably fast-flowing river and, although it may often look peaceful and serene, when in spate it becomes a roaring torrent and the water level can rise very rapidly and cause dangerous floods. Swaledale has many steep, branching valleys or gills to explore, such as Whitsundale, West Stonesdale, Oxnop and Gunnerside gills. The biggest side valley is Arkengarthdale, broader and more expansive than Swaledale and drained by Arkle Beck which joins the Swale at Reeth.

On the 26th August 1986, during the passage of Hurricane Charley, Arkle Beck rose twelve feet (3.6m) above normal during torrential rain. The river became a frightening and powerful force of destruction. Additional floodwater poured down Great Punchard Gill into the Arkle, and a surge of water hit Whaw Bridge, washing the top of it away. Outbuildings and hundreds of yards of walls and fences were destroyed, and silt from the leadmines was scattered on grazing land. Cottages in Langthwaite had floodwater knee-deep on the ground floors and, further downstream, the waters of the Swale surged round caravans at Grinton, threatening to carry them away. It would appear to be an unusual occurrence, but Harry Speight, writing in 1897 about flooding of the Swale, said:

'On several occasions the dale has been a complete wreck from end to end. During one of the floods a few years ago it was estimated that in many places in the dale fully 1,000 tons of debris covered each acre of land, while scarcely a bridge and wall for twenty miles were left standing.'

Geology of the Dale

Behind the scenery are the layers of sedimentary rocks which stick out here and there in natural scars, in the beds of rivers or by waterfalls. The geology of the dale is uncomplicated, and there is much to attract the walker who is interested in the physical landscape and the rocks which shape it. The Great Scar limestone is completely buried and it is the Yoredale series of rocks which line the sides of the dale, above which lie the Millstone Grit moors.

The Yoredales A thick sandwich of alternating limestones, sandstones and softer shales make up the Yoredales. These rocks were studied and named 160 years ago by the great Yorkshire geologist John Phillips, who was the first to understand how they were formed and how they affected the scenery. The repeated nature of the strata can be seen on the sides of the dale and in the gills, where the hard sandstones and limestones often form steps in the landscape. However, the limestone scars and stepped hillsides are less obvious than in Wensleydale. There are seven limestones in the series, the lowest to be exposed being the Hardraw limestone, on which Feetham is built. They can be seen in the side gills, for example, in Gunnerside Gill (*walk 14*) where the Hardraw limestone, Simonstone limestone and Middle limestones all occur in the scars along the valley sides. In Swinner Gill (*walk 18*), five of the limestones with related sandstones and shales are well exposed in this impressive, steep-sided ravine. The Underset limestone forms the beautiful waterfall of Kisdon Force at Keld, the village of Keld being on the Main limestone. Yoredale limestones are thinner and a little darker than the Great Scar limestones to the south, but often are rich in fossils such as lamp shells, corals and crinoid stems (sealilies). The total thickness of the Yoredales is about 1,000 feet (300m).

The ancient environment Corals need warm tropical seas in which to live and during Carboniferous times, some 340 million years ago, the climate was much warmer. The area now occupied by the North of England was then a shallow sea near the Equator, gradually being filled in by rivers bringing sand and mud from a former mountain region where Scotland now lies. Where they entered the sea, rivers splayed out into vast deltas. Every now and again the sea advanced on the land and, in the clear tropical seas, only the soft limey deposits of the droppings of shellfish, shell fragments, sea lilies and a few corals settled on the seabed. Then, as the sea became shallower, mud from the rivers reached the area, with a different fauna becoming established. Coiled goniatites (forerunners of the ammonite) did not mind the muddy conditions, and their fossil remains are found in the shales and are useful in dating the strata.

Near the margin of the land, sandbanks built up, sometimes to sea level when they carried a vegetation of primitive trees, such as the scale tree and giant horsetail. Occasionally there was enough forest vegetation to form beds of peat many feet thick. A few giant amphibians wandered through the undergrowth, leaving their footprints in the sand, while large dragonflies flew overhead. Then, over a short period of time, the land sank (or sea level rose) and clear seas covered the region again, corals and lamp shells colonising the seabed. Geologists call this a cyclothem, a sequence of events which was repeated several times during the deposition of the Yoredales, between about 340 and 330 million years ago.

Over a long period of time and squeezed beneath more thick deposits, the limey soup, soft mud, silts and sands slowly lost their seawater and turned to hard limestones, shales and sandstones. The peat layers were compressed to less than a tenth of their original thickness and, with the help of a certain amount of heat – from deep burial – turned to coal.

Fossils Apart from the usual corals and shells, there are two rather strange fossils you could keep an eye open for. They are common in Swaledale but rare elsewhere.

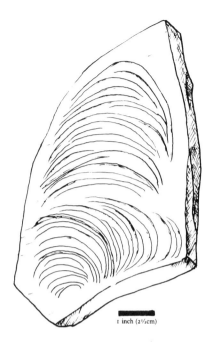

1 inch (2½cm)

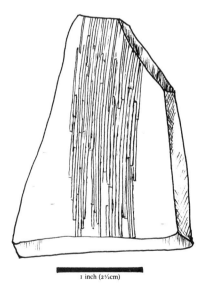

1 inch (2½cm)

Two fossils: Zoophycos, *a feeding burrow system, and the fossil sponge* Hyalostelia smithi.

One represents the feeding burrow of a creature called *Zoophycos*, which has left sweeping, curved traces across the rock. They occur, for example, on the path out of Swinner Gill up East Grain (*walk 15*) and in Slei Gill (*walk 8*). The other is a fossil sponge – or rather the long straight fibres that belonged to a sponge called *Hyalostelia* – and looks like a bunch of coarse bristles several inches long. Both fossils occur above the Main limestone and especially in the Richmond chert beds. I have found the sponge remains on Low Moor near Richmond (*walk 2*) and in Shaw Beck (*walk 4*).

Limestone scenery Because each of the Yoredale limestones is never very thick – most are less than twenty feet (6m) in thickness – there is no scenery one can call 'limestone country' (as in the Ingleborough area) and there are few potholes, caves and underground passages. However, at the top of the Yoredale series of rocks, the Main limestone is a prominent band. It averages seventy-five feet (23m) thick, reaches 130 feet (40m) on Kisdon and is responsible for several prominent scars and limestone features.

At the head of the dale are the Buttertubs, five potholes by the side of the road running from Thwaite over to Hawes. They appear rather unexpectedly in an otherwise bare moorland landscape. The two best lie one on each side of the road, so they are easy to visit. They are about 60 feet (19m) deep and have a complicated shape where the Main limestone has been sculptured and fluted by streamlets of acid-charged waters from the peaty moors above. Water from the potholes emerges in Cliff Beck just below the Buttertubs.

The distinctive limestone cliffs of Cotterby Scar near Keld (*walk 19*), Kisdon and Ivelet scars above Muker (*walk 15*) and of course the high scar of Fremington Edge (*walk 7*) are all formed by the Main

3

The head of Swaledale: Keld and East Stonesdale, with High Pike and High Seat in the background.

limestone. The path to Nine Standards Rigg (*walk 20*) crosses a rare Swaledale limestone pavement on Tailbridge Hill near the watershed with the Eden Valley. The Main limestone here lies 1,700 feet (520m) above sea level, which contrasts with 330 feet (100m) altitude at Richmond Castle 22½ miles (36km) away. The gentle dip of the strata is in fact to the north-east. Where you have such a mixture of rock types, limestone supports a bright green turf with a great variety of flowering plants, a contrast to the coarser grasses on sandstones and shales.

Millstone Grit On top of the multiple sandwich of Yoredale rocks comes the Millstone Grit, a series of coarse sandstones with intervening shales and occasional coals. The gritstone caps the moors to the north and south of the dale and, because of the lack of any limestone and because of the flat-lying arrangement of the strata, forms widespread, fairly horizontal acid moors, broadly covered with heather, cotton grass and sphagnum bog.

The biggest coal seam – over three feet (1m) thick – is the Tan Hill coal in the lower part of the Millstone Grit, which was

Kisdon Gorge between Keld and Muker (seen here from Beldi Hill) was formed when torrents of water from a melting Ice Age glacier cut this deep and secluded valley, the Swale's former course to the west of Kisdon being blocked by glacial debris.

worked for centuries on the moors near Tan Hill and helped fuel the hungry lead-smelting mills. Other coal seams occur below the Underset and Main limestones; they vary in quality and thickness, and have been mined locally for lime-burning and domestic use.

Minerals Perhaps the most interesting aspect of the geology of Swaledale is the mineralisation that has taken place, especially on the north side of the valley between Keld and Arkengarthdale, where there is a concentration of east-west faults which the mineral veins occupy.

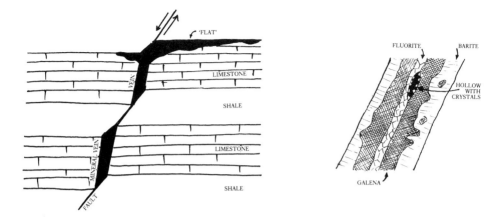

The formation of a mineral vein. Movement along a fault produces open spaces for vein minerals to occupy. Right: *a rich vein about twenty inches (50cm) across.*

About 300 million years ago, after the rocks of the area had become fairly solid, there appears to have been a re-heating of the granite mass which today is centred under Wensleydale. This was the heat source that activated the movement of hot brines which carried elements such as fluorine, barium and lead to penetrate the sedimentary layers above. The expanding hot granite also pushed gently upwards, cracking the rocks above and making room for the in-filling of the mineral veins. The temperature of the fluid varied between 100 and 150°C and affected mainly the Underset and Main limestones, where calcite, barite, witherite, fluorite and galena crystallised out. In some places the ores of zinc and copper were deposited and, further down the dale near Richmond, copper was mined in the early years of this century (*walk 3*). Remains of the great age of leadmining, the old workings, spoil heaps and hushes, can be seen on many of the walks (*see also the next chapter*).

Galena is the ore of lead (lead sulphide) and occurs in veins which may be traced for several miles. A workable quantity of galena is called an oreshoot which is usually of no great extent, being present in a ribbon or string a few inches wide. There was no guarantee for the miner of what lay ahead: the ore could be regular, or it could swell into a large mass or thin out to nothing. Where the ore died out, the miners may have kept digging along the vein in the hope of another rich find, and there are stories of how mining was halted just short of the ore which could have made their fortunes. Sometimes the ore is formed in flats, a large mass at the side of a vein where some of the limestone has been replaced by the ore, and these include the richest deposits. It was often pure luck for miners to come across a flat, several of which have been mined on Grinton Moor. The miners only wanted the galena and the white sparry minerals were thrown out. The old lead-mine tip heaps are full of interesting specimens and often tracks are surfaced with leadmine tailings, so there is a good chance of being able to identify the most common.

Lumps of barite or barytes (barium sulphate) are particularly heavy and have a platy structure or a fine 'cock's comb' crystal form. The barite which occurs along the track near Flincher Gill and Forefield Rake (*walk 14*) is a beautiful pink instead of the usual white. Another barium mineral is witherite (carbonate rather than sulphate) which is rare except in Swaledale. The whitish crystals form pyramids or a fibrous arrangement. They look glassy, a bit like quartz, but are heavy and can be scratched with a knife. Fluorite is also rather watery-looking and heavyish, but often displays cubic crystals and may be green or yellow in colour. Calcite is a common mineral of lead veins, usually white, will scratch with a copper coin and fizzes when a drop of very dilute hydrochloric acid is applied. Occasionally you may come across pearly dolomite crystals, which have the distinction of curved faces.

Glacial features   In geologically more recent times, the great Ice Age in Britain has seen the ice advance on several occasions in the last million years or so. However, the last ice sheet, which existed between 26,000 and 10,000 years ago, obliterated all the evidence of earlier ice sheets and glaciers, and is the one responsible for the many glacial features that now remain. Swaledale, like the other Yorkshire Dales, was ridden over by a thick sheet of ice which was level with the highest peaks, though, like the others, the dale developed its own glacier. The ice smoothed the contours, broadened the valley and stripped away loose debris, depositing most of it lower down and even diverting the course of the River Swale at Keld and Round Howe.

Some 13,000 or 14,000 years ago, the Swaledale ice was in retreat as the climate started to warm a little; the glacier was melting faster than it was moving forward. The debris it was carrying was dropped at its snout at intervals along the valley to form what are known as terminal moraines. For a time, each moraine formed a dam across the valley with a lake ponded up behind it. But eventually the river cut through the moraines and drained the lakes. What is left of four moraines can be seen below Gunnerside Bridge, above Low Whita Bridge, below Grinton Bridge and by Ellerton Abbey. The former lake beds are now mainly meadows or poorly-drained fields, still flooded occasionally in the winter. At Usha Gap near Thwaite, the disturbed slopes north of the river are those of an old landslide and the mounds near the river look like another terminal moraine.

Waterfalls   The distinctive and endearing scenery of Swaledale is enhanced by the many waterfalls. Six or seven cluster round Keld, and you can discover many on the side gills in Birkdale, at Ravenseat, in Swinner Gill, upper Gunnerside Gill, Hard Level Gill and Marske Beck. They are at their best when there is plenty of water in them, so make the most of rainy days – like the Victorian topographer Harry Speight, who wrote:

'To see them all in flood with their white tails galloping down the mist-screened hills and craggy steeps, and the amber-foamed cataracts leaping madly in the valley below, is to witness a scene truly Alpine in its wild and forbidding grandeur.'

Near Keld, the Swale throws itself over the stepped falls of Hoggarths Leap, surges over Catrake Force, enters a narrow gorge next to the village, is joined by East Gill which tumbles over the scenic East Gill

The waterfalls of Kisdon Force pour through a deep rocky gorge just below Keld.

Force and drops over the two falls of Kisdon Force. The last two can be seen on walk 17 together with those of Swinner Gill. There is a lovely waterfall in Ellas's Stot Wood above Ivelet and another in Cliff Beck (seen from the road near Thwaite), both exciting spectacles after heavy rain. Hard Level Force (*walk 12*) and Orgate Force (*walk 4*) are impressive, and you will see many others like those high up Gunnerside Gill or above Pillimire Bridge on Marske Beck. Waterfalls are interesting places for the naturalist. They often have a secluded gorge below them and may harbour a fascinating collection of shade- and water-loving plants.

MAN AND THE LANDSCAPE

After the ice had gone from the Dales, the valleys and uplands became covered in vegetation. Glacial lakes and marshes on the valley floor gave way on the lower slopes to forests of alder and ash where wolves and bears roamed. On the higher ground, even over the tops, grew a woodland of birch, hazel and pine where there were red deer, wild ox and mountain goats. From this time, man was to have a striking influence on the landscape, which at first was changed only in small ways, but it was an influence which accelerated as time went on.

Prehistory The first indication of man in Swaledale are finds of flints of Mesolithic Age (8000-6000 BC) and flint arrowheads of Neolithic times (2500 BC to 1800 BC), but signs of settlement in the dale come with the Bronze Age people, who arrived about 1800 BC, with further influxes between 1500 and 1000 BC. The climate was pleasantly dry and warm, and these people chose to live well up the valley sides where the forest was less dense and there were good views along the dale. Such a place is Arngill Scar (*walk 15*), overlooking Kisdon gorge above Muker, where human bones have been discovered, and on Harkerside where there is a small stone circle. The great earthwork of Maiden Castle on Harkerside has also been ascribed to the Bronze Age, though its detailed history still remains a mystery.

Maiden Castle (*walk 6*) is one of the biggest and most impressive of all the prehistoric monuments in the Yorkshire Dales yet, until excavated, nobody will know for certain who built it or what it was used for. A huge ditch, fifteen feet (4.5m) deep, has been carved out of the hillside in a rough pear shape, 120 by 100 yards (110×90m), with a long entrance in the form of an avenue of stones. There are traces of hut circles within it. So, was it a defensive fort against the Romans, along with the ramparts on the east end of Harkerside, or was it a genuine settlement with its own defences? Most recent thinking suggests it is the latter and is pre-Roman. The paths leading to it and alongside it are indistinct, and the earthwork is covered in coarse heather and bracken which disguises its bold shape.

During the last ten years, archaeologists have been studying the dale and making many new discoveries. Research is revealing that that the Bronze Age and Iron Age populations in the dale were much greater than was thought. There are remains of settlements on both sides of the valley, on the slopes of Calver Hill, near Reeth, and across on Harkerside where old field patterns, wall boundaries, house platforms and lanes, of Iron Age and Romano-British times, are being mapped in detail. When fully revealed, the prehistory of Swaledale is likely to prove a rich and fascinating story.

The large embankments which run down Harkerside (*walk 6*) and which can be traced onto Fremington Edge (*walk 7*) are believed to have been a defensive position across the valley for the Brigantes, in their struggle against the Romans. Other Iron Age earthworks occur on How Hill, at Low Whita and on the Grinton moraine, both of which were then islands of dry land in a marshy area, and so good defensive sites. The excavated settlement under Whitcliffe Scar was occupied in post-Roman times up to AD 600.

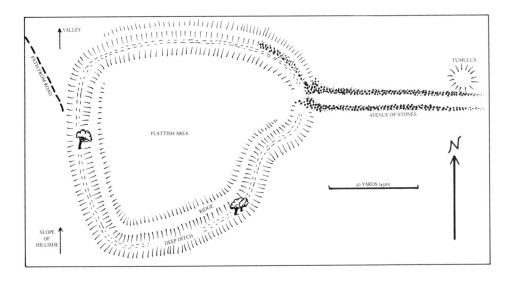

VALLEY

PATH FROM ROAD

TUMULUS

AVENUE OF STONES

FLATTISH AREA

N

50 YARDS (45m)

SLOPE
OF
HILLSIDE

RIDGE

DEEP DITCH

A plan of Maiden Castle on Harkerside: an Iron Age, pre-Roman defensive site.

The Romans Cataractonium was the great fort at Catterick, and it was not far from the leadmines of Swaledale. Two pigs (large heavy ingots) of lead have been found in the dale bearing Roman inscriptions (since lost), as well as some fragments of pottery and a bronze horse-harness (in York Museum). The pig at Hurst had the name 'Hadrian' on it, and was found with wooden shovels and other tools in an old working, broken into during mining. It is thought that the Brigantes worked as slaves in the Hurst mines. The Romans must have visited and crossed the dale, but there is no evidence of their roads, villas or forts.

Anglian and Norse settlement In the year 625, Christianity came to Northumbria when Bishop Paulinus, the first Archbishop of York, baptised thousands of people in the River Swale, probably at Catterick. Swaledale may not have been settled until about the eighth century when

the Angles founded communities in the lower dale at Reeth, Stainton, Grinton and Fremington. The *ton* was a family farmstead, to become the focus of a hamlet or village as the population grew. The people had a co-operative open field system of farming, and the homesteads were grouped round an area where cattle could be safely kept, which later became the village green, like the large one in Reeth.

At the beginning of the tenth century the Norse Vikings came across the Pennines, by way of Ireland and the Lake District, to settle the upper part of the dale. The land was empty and they required grazing land on the fells above the forest level. They made clearings among the trees, and in summer took their sheep and cattle to the *shielings* or summer pastures. There are many Old Norse names in upper Swaledale, especially on the sunny northern side, which include Ravenseat, Keld, Thwaite, Muker, Gunnerside and Melbecks. The placename elements 'seat' and 'side' come from *saetr* – meaning *shieling* or summer farm – *keld* is a spring and *thwaite* a sloping clearing. Beck, dale, foss and gill are all Norse words. The people were tough and independent, and their farms or long-houses were widely-scattered. The remains of a longhouse above Gunnerside village may be the original 'Gunnar's *shieling*'.

The Normans With the arrival of William the Conquerer, there was a threat of rebellion in the North, and William replied in 1069 by a campaign of destruction in which all houses, crops, grain, cattle and food were burnt. Thousands of people were killed or starved to death, while others tried to leave the area or were forced to eat dogs and cats or even human flesh to stay alive. The region between York and Durham was almost uninhabited for a time, and Swaledale became a backwater for several decades. The *Domesday* survey in 1086 described most of the villages in the North Riding as 'waste'.

William built castles to establish his power over the people. For his hand in subduing the English, Count Alan of Brittany was granted the Honour of Richmond. The massive fortress at Richmond was one of the first stone castles in the land (built between 1071 and 1091). It was a military base, so the best defensive position was chosen on a bluff, overlooking the Swale and the plains beyond. The walled town was built soon after the *Domesday* survey in 1086, when the castle bailey became the focus for the new town. The huge keep was built in 1146 and still dominates the sky-line. The large cobbled market place in which stands a church is all part of the original Continental design. Much of Swaledale became a Norman hunting forest under Robert Arkhil, whose name was given to Arkle Beck and Arkengarth-

dale. Upper Swaledale became the manor of Healaugh under Walter de Gant, kins-man to William. The Reeth area continued to be farmed, and terraces – or strip lynchets – were worked in an extension of cropland up the sides of the valley during a warm period in the thirteenth century. It was easier to plough by turning the earth downhill and always in the same direction. Repeated ploughing, together with the working of land in strips, gradually formed the terraces.

Monasteries and nunneries At the time of William the Conquerer there was a period of strong religious enthusiasm and of monastery building. The first in Swale-dale was the Benedictine priory of St Martin, built across the river from Rich-mond Castle, of which there are still some remains (*walk 1*). In 1151 the Premon-stratensians built the abbey of St Agatha at Easby half a mile (800m) away on the left bank of the river. The white canons were here for nearly 400 years, and influenced the local community as they were con-cerned not just with preaching, but work in the parish, education and offering hos-pitality to travellers. The picturesque and extensive ruins of Easby are situated in a beautiful spot by the Swale (*walk 1*). Further up the dale, Marrick Priory, built about 1154, was a Benedictine foundation (*walk 5*) which housed black-robed nuns and lay sisters, and at Ellerton Priory on the other side of the Swale were a small num-ber of white-habited Cistercian nuns.

During the monastic times Richmond prospered, as did the wool trade and the religious houses. But in the fourteenth century the Scots raided and plundered as far south as the Yorkshire Dales, including York. Marrick Priory was attacked in 1318, and Ellerton had its charters and writings destroyed when raided in 1347. In 1349 the plague spread from the port of Hull, the

Easby Church is older than the nearby abbey of the same name, and the site may date from AD 700.

economy did not recover for generations and Easby became the site of a plague cemetery. The Dissolution and closing of the monasteries started in 1536, but there were many ordinary people who did not want the changes and who supported the Pilgrimage of Grace. This was a rebellion against the closure by those who depended on the monasteries for their livelihood, people who would lose their jobs or their trade. When it was suppressed, leaders like Francis Bigod of Healaugh Manor and Anthony Peacock of Arkengarthdale were captured and executed. In the novel, *The Man on a Donkey*, H F M Prescott gives colour and background to the story of Marrick Priory in the 1530s.

Churches Two outstanding churches of the dale are those of Grinton and Easby. St Andrews of Grinton (*walk 6*) is known as the 'Cathedral of the Dales', perhaps because of its lofty and dignified interior. It has a Norman font and a stained glass window of St George and the dragon. It was founded in Norman times by the monks of Bridlington Priory, and was the parish church for the whole of the upper dale. Funeral cortèges from the head of the dale travelled up to twelve miles (19km) along the Corpse Road, until Muker had its own church and burial ground in 1580. Easby Church, dedicated to St Agatha, stands next to Easby Abbey (*walk 1*). It was the parish church before the abbey was built and still is today. It is full of interesting treasures, including fascinating thirteenth century wall paintings.

Farmhouses, barns and walls The old farmhouses and cottages often have a lintel over the door indicating the date and the initials of the people who first lived there. The earliest dates are seventeenth century – not as early as the other dales – and a house in Grinton is dated 1665, one in Gunnerside 1690 and one in Feetham, 1693. Rows of houses are characteristic of Swaledale, as in Low Row (*walk 13*). Houses and cottages were built onto a farmhouse which developed into a row, with the later buildings at each end. Many of these would be owned by miners who had only a small plot of land. Many of the farms in the upper dale are typical long-houses, with living quarters and barn all under one roof.

The small field barns, one in almost every meadow, are a special feature of the Swaledale landscape. The barns housed three or four young cows and their feed hay through the winter. The hay was also used for sheep, brought down from the fells in the hardest part of the winter. The attractive pattern of field walls and barns is well seen near Gunnerside (*walk 13*) and Muker (*walk 16*).

The older drystone walls enclose small irregular fields near to the villages, and these date from the sixteenth or seventeenth century. The first to be enclosed by Act of Parliament were on Fremington Edge in 1778. Thomas Elliot of Fremington Hall was the enthusiast behind it and he was described as 'one of the greatest improvers of moors in Yorkshire'. By the late eighteenth century, higher ground was being enclosed by a series of straight parallel walls. The enclosures allowed big takeovers of common land by the gentry, taking away grazing rights from the poorer farmers. Contrast the small fields below Angram with the large rectangular shapes higher up on Angram Pasture.

However, life in Swaledale was always slower and more remote from the law. The result is that, unlike Wharfedale or Wensleydale, there are large tracts of land on each side of the dale that have never been enclosed. The wall which borders open country and lies furthest from the farm is known as the intake wall.

Packhorse routes, drove roads and miners' tracks For centuries, pack-horses were the main form of transport and were used in the mining areas up to the 1880s. A train was made up of twenty or thirty ponies each carrying a load of 250 lbs (114kg) in a pair of panniers or wooden pack saddle. A wooden frame on the pony's back, called a crutch, was used for light and bulky loads like bales of wool. The most commonly used ponies in the Dales were bred from the hardy German Jaeger or hunter ponies, and the name Jagger still survives in placenames, such as Jagger Lane north of Richmond, and in surnames.

Where the route crossed a river, it was usual to ford it, but if the riverbank was steep, then a single arch bridge was built. The finest bridge in Swaledale is the pack-horse bridge at Ivelet (*walk 16*); others include the one at Ravenseat (*walk 19*) and Pillimire Bridge (*walk 4*) near Marske. There are coal roads which radiate from Tan Hill, and lead roads from the mining areas which followed the old Richmond road on the north side of the river and north along Jagger Lane to Hartforth (*walk 2*). A network of miners' tracks was in use on a local scale, well seen in Gunnerside Gill (*walk 14*) and near Old Gang Mine (*walk 12*).

A major drove road crossed the dale from the Scottish borders on its way south to fairs at Askrigg, Appletreewick and

Malham Moor. It entered upper Arkengarthdale via Dale Head and Whaw (*walk 9*) and crossed the Arkle at Stang Bridge. Nearby was a drover's inn called Lilly Jocks. The road continued over to Surrender Bridge (*walks 11 and 12*) and reached Swaledale at Feetham, crossing probably at Isles Bridge (*walk 13*) to traverse Summer Lodge Moor to Askrigg. In about 1800, when the droving trade was at its peak, some 10,000 cattle a year were being driven south into England, and most of them came through the Dales. This continued until the 1890s when refrigeration allowed fresh meat to be imported cheaply.

Leadmining As a result of man's insatiable demand for lead, dramatic changes, to the point of devastation, were wrought upon the landscape. On the northern side of the dale between Keld and Hurst (*walks 7, 8, 11, 12, 14 and 15*) there is a greater concentration of old leadmines than in any other part of the Dales. Ruined buildings, spoil heaps, hushes, giant flues and mine entrances are scattered across the countryside. The miners followed veins in the Underset and Main limestones in a hectic search for the ore. When they came across old mine workings, they always spoke of them knowingly as 't'owd man', in the singular, referring to the toil of previous generations of miners.

Lead may have been one reason for the Roman presence in Britain. In the twelfth century, lead from Swaledale was ordered for the Tower of London, Dover Castle and Jervaulx Abbey. You could even buy the commodity on Richmond market where it was taxed 'two pence for every cartload'.

The extraction of lead ore involved the technique of 'hushing'. Even the Romans used this system, which was developed on a grand scale in the eighteenth century. Turf dams were built to collect as much water as possible, which was then released in a torrent down the hillside to expose the vein. A sluice allowed repeated use of the dam and, after the surface soil and rubble was scoured away, the miners would loosen any ore with picks. The next flood of water would then trap the ore in a deep pit dug along the course of the hush. The hushes now appear as deep gashes on the hillsides, and are very noticeable on the sides of Gunnerside Gill (*walk 14*).

The big expansion in leadmining started at the beginning of the eighteenth century with new methods of production. Tunnels into the hillside, known as adits or levels, allowed the use of rails with men or ponies to heave the tubs. Water, which had always been such a problem, could drain out and air circulation was improved. The ore, mixed with the waste minerals like barite, fluorite, and limestone, had to be separated out. It was crushed by machine, or broken up by women and boys with hammers on the 'dressing' floor; then it was shaken on racks under a flow of water so that the ore sank to the bottom and the lighter rock and spar came to the top.

The smelt mills relied on water power and so were usually situated downstream from the mines where a large waterwheel worked the bellows for the furnace. The ore was lead sulphide, so all that was required was heat and the presence of carbon to separate the metal from the sulphur, which was given off as fumes. The long flues up the hillsides greatly improved the draught for the furnace and at the same time the lead and oxide of lead, which condensed on the sides of the flue, could be retrieved. This work was done by boys who crawled up the flue and scraped off the deposits. At the peak of the industry there were forty smelt mills in Swaledale and Arkengarthdale. The remains at Old Gang and Surrender Bridge are being stabilised and preserved (*walks 11 and 12*). Both have long flues which can be traced up the hill-

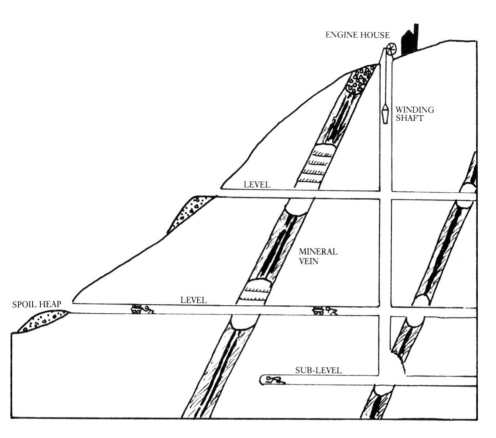

ENGINE HOUSE

WINDING
SHAFT

LEVEL

MINERAL
VEIN

SPOIL HEAP

LEVEL

SUB-LEVEL

How a leadmine works.

side and in which there is some remarkable arched stonework.

For the miner, life was hard and often cut short by a mining accident or by lung diseases. In the mid-nineteenth century, the life expectancy for a miner in Swaledale was only 46, but 61 for all other occupations. He had to walk a few miles to the mine over wild moorland, exposed to wind and rain. When he arrived his clothes may have been soaked, and he then had to struggle down ladders and along dark damp tunnels to his working place underground, where candlelight was the only illumin-

ation. Bad air was often a problem in dead-end levels, adding to the hazardous conditions. At the end of the day the miner would trudge home, often chilled to the bone by cold winds. The London Lead Company tried to reduce the dangers from respiratory diseases by the provision of smallholdings and encouraging miners to spend more time in the open air. One legacy the miners left is the maze of footpaths, many of which are now rights of way.

In Billy Bank Wood near Richmond, copper was worked from 1906 to 1915 and

Gunnerside Gill, at the junction with Blind Gill (left), showing Blakethwaite smelt mill and peat house.

this may have been the location of the fifteenth century 'Richmond Copper Mines' referred to in a charter of Edward IV in 1454. According to R T Clough, a smelt mill for copper was built here in 1585 which would support this assertion. Today, entrances to two adits can be seen near the riverbank and signs of the green copper minerals malachite and chrysocolla occur along the path (*walk 3*).

Farming and grouse-shooting The attractive present-day scenery of Swaledale has evolved by centuries of pastoral farming. Most farms have sheep with a few cows, and it is the keeping of cows that is responsible for the scenic field barns and flowery meadows in the bottom of the

valley. Sheep also affected the landscape by their constant grazing which did not allow young trees to survive, so the moors and fells today are treeless.

Wool has been a valuable product since monastic times, and the wealth of Britain once depended on it. Most of the sheep in the dale and on the fells are of the hardy Swaledale breed, with their familiar black faces and pale grey noses. They are particularly valuable in that they can stand the harsh conditions of the uplands in winter, and flocks can be trained with 'a sense of belonging' to keep to their own part of the fell. They produce good quality white wool of medium length, traditionally used in carpets but also in hard-wearing worsteds and tweeds. Knitting has recently been

Limestone was burnt in field limekilns like this one in Gunnerside Gill, and the lime was spread on fields to improve the soil, or used to make mortar.

revived in the dale, and thick sweaters made from local wool are sold at a cottage shop in Muker. When crossed with 'mutton' sheep such as Leicesters and Wensleydales, Swaledales produce good fat lambs for lowland farmers. A good Swaledale ram or tup can be worth thousands of pounds. Agricultural shows still take place in Reeth and Muker in late August and early September, and the May fair at the Tan Hill Inn (*walk 20*) is *the* show for Swaledale sheep.

One particular pursuit with its own effect on the landscape is grouse-shooting. It is a sport that has been carried on in Swaledale for 150 years, and is now big business on the large estates. Careful management has not only produced some of the broadest stretches of heather moor in the Dales, but

also given a chequered appearance to many parts of it. Walkers will notice a patchwork of greys and greens where blocks of heather have been systematically burned, to encourage the growth of new young shoots, the main food of the red grouse. Lines of shooting butts, some solidly constructed of stone, appear in even the remotest of places and are made to tone in with the surroundings. More easily seen are the new roads built across the fells, enabling the grouse-shooting parties to reach the butts and shooting huts in four-wheel-drive vehicles.

People A history of Swaledale reveals a multitude of interesting people: great landlords like the Swales and the Whartons, mine owners with their feuds and

17

bankruptcies, outstanding characters such as Robert Willance and Captain Harland, and famous names such as the Kearton brothers.

The dale was a Nonconformist stronghold. The Quakers had many followers and built meeting houses in Healaugh, Smarber and Low Row; in Reeth they also built a school. John Wesley's message was one the miners understood well; the Methodist chapels they built held hundreds, while Anglican churches almost fell into ruin.

During Victorian times, Swaledale experienced a depopulation and migration greater than any of the other dales. The population of the dale (excluding Richmond) reached its peak of 8,279 in 1821, and started a gradual decline which accelerated dramatically after 1851 so that by 1901 it was down to 3,061. The mining industry had attracted a large influx of people with, at its peak, more workers in mining than in farming, but the nineteenth century saw growing difficulties in the industry, which finally collapsed by the 1880s. People started leaving about 1825, but particularly in the 1840s and many later, after the Crimean War. The mines were made deeper and the ore became more difficult and more expensive to extract, and by the 1870s imported ore from Spain and South America was much cheaper. The dale lost almost half its people between 1871 and 1891. Many left to settle and make a good living in North America – some to work in the leadmines of Iowa, Illinois and Wisconsin – others went to mines in Spain and a large number to Lancashire, the men finding work in the coal pits and the women in the cotton mills.

Apart from a visit by Turner, and later writings by Speight and Bogg, Swaledale remained largely unknown and of little interest to most people. Even in the 1930s, when Ella Pontefract and Marie Hartley published their trilogy of books, this outstanding dale was still peaceful and seldom visited. In 1954, the beauty of the whole region became officially recognised and considered worthy of conservation, when the Yorkshire Dales were designated a National Park.

The present-day scenery of Swaledale combines the ancient geology and glacial history with the work of man. In fact, man has had such an influence on the landscape that it could be thought of as a by-product of the work of the many peoples involved: the Iron Age and Anglian settlers, the monks and their flocks, the drovers and jaggers, 't'owd man' of the mines and all the small farmers down the ages. All have unknowingly participated in the creation of a precious and wonderful part of the British countryside, scenery that no one person could ever have devised. Today, the only survivor of those landscape artists is the hill farmer, and if the beauty of the dale is going to last, then future conservation will be closely linked with farming. The National Park is the custodian but the farmers will be the stewards. They will need all our help and encouragement.

WILDLIFE

Swaledale is a rewarding area for bird-watching, with a good variety of species. Habitats include large heather-covered moors, many rocky gills, a few patches of woodland and flower-rich river meadows. There are no wide stretches of open water to attract waterfowl, with the exception of the reserve at Bolton-on-Swale below Richmond, but the river attracts a number of water birds. A great deal of enjoyment can be had by the interested visitor with a pair of binoculars and time to spare. Patience is essential, as species are very local and must be looked for. There are several birds of prey that frequent the area.

Birds such as the peregrine falcon and hen harrier have returned in small numbers only in the last twenty years, after being infrequent visitors.

While out walking keep an eye open, too, for mammals. You can usually catch sight of a furry individual, perhaps a stoat or roe deer, at any time of year, and in the spring and summer there are several species of butterflies to look out for.

Birdwatching Localities:

Heather moors (*walks 4, 6, 10, 12, 15 and 20*) The most extensive habitat in Swaledale is the heather moorland which stretches out to the horizon on both sides of the valley. The underlying rock is Millstone Grit, the soils are acid and the dominant plant is ling or common heather. Most of the moors are managed specifically for

The redstart prefers open woodland or overgrown hedgerows, and often nests in a drystone wall.

grouse-shooting and protection of the heather, especially the growth of young green shoots which are encouraged by burning. There is a record of grouse being shot in Swaledale 250 years ago, though the sport only developed in the mid-nineteenth century, and since then Parliament has traditionally started its summer break in time for the grouse season beginning on the 'Glorious Twelfth' (of August).

One of the best birdwatching moors is Reeth High Moor which culminates in Great Pinseat (*walk 12*). Heather is the natural habitat of the merlin, where you may see it flying fast and close to the ground, twisting and turning as it chases a meadow pipit or skylark. This small falcon is a wary bird and not easy to spot, though may be seen perching on a rock or hummock. Another bird of the moors and sometimes prey to the merlin is the ring ouzel. Its piping *pee-u* call is worth listening for, though when disturbed it gives a loud scolding *chaka-chaka*. The sooty black male has a white crescent on the throat, the female being a browner grey with a less clearly marked crescent. In late summer they start to leave the uplands to winter in southern Europe. A bird which also likes to be near heather is the strikingly handsome golden plover. Its plaintive whistling call is one of the most beautiful sounds of the moors and will help to locate it. Its gold-speckled back shines in the sun and contrasts with the pale-bordered black belly. You may see groups on the wing by mid-summer, with their fast flight and rapid wingbeats.

It is wonderful to see the short-eared owl as it hunts close to the ground, flapping along like a huge pale moth, its sensitive ears picking out the faintest rustle in the grass. The main prey is the field vole, and when there is an increase in the vole population a large brood of young owls can be reared. You can expect to see snipe on

A golden plover stands sentinel.

Reeth High Moor, either by disturbing them, when they take off in a hurried twisting flight, or when they are 'drumming' high in the air. They like to be near boggy ground or shallow water, where they probe for worms. Lapwing and curlew are two other birds which can be seen on many of the moors, though not necessarily on the highest peaks, and twite seem limited to Harkerside (*walk 6*) and Hurst Moors (*walk 7*). Calver Hill (*walk 10*) is also a haunt of golden plover, snipe, lapwing and curlew.

Hen harriers, peregrines and buzzards all breed in the Swaledale area, but are sadly still subjected to persecution on some moors. I was lucky enough to see a male hen harrier near the summit of Great Pinseat (*walk 12*) as it hunted along a dip in the heather, looking white with black wingtips as it flew lazily along. The male is in fact pale grey above and white below, whereas the female, a little larger than the male, is brown above and streaked below with a white rump. A few seconds later, in another direction, I watched as a peregrine, after circling a couple of times, 'stooped' in a headlong dive to the ground. The prey is killed by a blow from its powerful talons. The buzzard is the largest bird of the open moors and may be seen particularly in the spring and autumn, soaring over limestone scars or moving along in an effortless flight as it searches for small mammals, especially rabbits.

Rocky gills (*walks 4, 8, 11, 12, 14, 16, 17 and 19*) Steep, rocky ravines, or gills, are a feature of the side streams of Swaledale. The scenery is wild and impressive, where steep slopes and cliffs overlook the beck which tumbles far below, over rock ledges and waterfalls. Such a place is the upper part of Gunnerside Gill (*walk 14*) and another is Slei Gill (*walk 8*) in Arkengarthdale. Both of these are excellent localities for the ring ouzel. On a spring walk up to Botcher Gill (off Gunnerside Gill) or the slopes of Slei Gill you can count five or six pairs of ring ouzel. This handsome bird is so common in the higher parts of the dale that the mountain blackbird, as it is sometimes called, could be considered an emblem of Swaledale. That little bird with the white rump, the wheatear, is common wherever there are plenty of rocks, old ruins or walls for it to find a nest site, and the steep gills are ideal for it. Arriving from its winter in Africa, in early April, the wheatear is a welcome sign of spring. Its name comes from the Anglo-Saxon *hwit* and *oers*, meaning 'white rump'.

As you walk up one of the small rushing becks, you are very likely to see the grey wagtail, an elegant grey and yellow bird with a black throat. It nests in a crevice in the bank or roots of a tree and is never far from fast-flowing water. The dipper, too, likes the rushing water and is found in the same habitat. This bird finds its food by walking underwater on the shallow stream bed. It is distinguished by its white shirt-front and chestnut waistband. The short tail and bobbing habit make it unmistakable.

Riverside (*walks 1, 3, 5, 6, 7, 13, 16 and 17*) Both the River Swale and Arkle Beck can produce a very interesting selection of birds at all times of the year. The Swale above and below the 'swing bridge' at Reeth is particularly rewarding for the birdwatcher. The shrill call of *kleep-kleep-kleep* announces the presence of the oyster-catcher which nests on patches of gravel, the nest being nothing more than a 'scrape' among the pebbles. A more musical, high-pitched call of *tsee-wee-wee* belongs to the common sandpiper. This small, rather dull-coloured wader blends in with the pebbles and stones, until it takes off in a low flight, calling as it goes. It is a common summer visitor all along the Swale and on many of the smaller tributaries.

Quite a different waterbird is the large goosander, which now breeds on the Swale in its spread south. The male's breeding plumage displays a handsome dark green head and pinkish-white body. The female's head is red-brown. Even from a distance the long, narrow red bill is distinctive and not at all duck-like. Where the river has cut a vertical sandy bank, the sand martin will exploit it by scraping out a tunnel two to

The curlew's haunting call is unmistakable, but it is a wary bird.

three feet (60-90cm) long, with an enlarged nest chamber at the end. You will hear the sand martins twittering as they wing to and fro over the water to catch insects. As well as in the rocky gills the grey wagtail also breeds along the river. It is a true waterbird and usually found near moving water.

For those who enjoy winter walks, this is the season when there is a good chance of seeing a kingfisher. A shy, beautiful bird, it is often seen as a flash of blue as it speeds along the river, changing to orange when it alights to face you. The main enemy of the kingfisher is a severe winter when streams and rivers freeze over. Long-tailed tits also succumb to severe weather, but groups of them may be seen with siskins feeding on

alders along the riverbank. The yellow-green siskin is rather like a greenfinch but smaller, with a black crown and chin and yellow wing-bar. The redshank, too, frequents the river in winter, its most distinguishing feature being the long orange-red legs and, in flight, the white wing-bar. The winter plumage is less strongly marked than in the spring. You may see the heron motionless at the water's edge as it waits patiently for an unsuspecting fish, quickly striking it with a long, sharp bill. You may also catch sight of a peregrine, too, along the river, and in spring look out for teal near Feetham (*walk 13*). This attractive little dabbling duck is with us all year but never common.

The common sandpiper is seen along the River Swale and its side-streams from mid-April.

Deciduous woodland (*walks 4, 5, 7, 8, 11, 13 and 14*) Woodlands of all types are small and limited along both Swaledale and Arkengarthdale, and the birds to be found there tend to be very local. There are several small patches of wood that can be rewarding, like those in Kisdon Gorge and Gunnerside Gill. Two important sites are Scar House Wood above Langthwaite (*walk 8*) and Steps Wood near Marrick Priory (*walk 5*). Both have a breeding population of warblers (chiffchaff, willow warbler, wood warbler, and blackcap) which visit us between April and October. A good musical ear is an advantage when sorting them out, though the willow warbler can easily be distinguished from the chiffchaff by its song, and the black crown of the blackcap and the yellow breast of the wood warbler are fairly distinctive. Great spotted woodpecker, green woodpecker and tree-creeper also breed in these two woods. Scar House also has the popular and handsome pied flycatcher and the colourful redstart.

Redstarts prefer the edge of the wood, and drystone walls make good nest sites. You may hear the *weet* sound before you see the chestnut red rump and tail. Nuthatch, garden warbler and spotted flycatcher are additional breeding birds in Steps Wood. The acrobatic nuthatch, with us all year, is another attractive small bird with a distinctive shape. It is the only bird to walk down a tree headfirst. The garden warbler is probably the ultimate 'little brown bird', with no distinguishing feature except for its tuneful song. But another brown bird, the spotted flycatcher, gives itself away by its behaviour: the way it dives for a fly and returns to its perch.

Meadows and farmland (*walks 2, 3, 5, 6, 7, 11, 13, 15, 16 and 17*) An extensive habitat along the valley floor and lower slopes is perhaps more famous for its wild flowers than its birds, but some interesting species breed here. The yellowhammer likes open places with hedgerows and few trees, and is thinly scattered in the farming area north of Richmond (*walk 2*). An even brighter yellow is the yellow wagtail which inhabits the broader floodplain of the Swale and may be seen near Reeth and Low Row (*walks 6 and 11*). You are almost sure to see the handsome redstart while out walking where there are a few trees or bushes for cover. In the same sort of habitat you may see another summer visitor, the tree pipit, conspicuous by its song flight. It flies up from a tree and parachutes down with wings and tail spread, delivering its song to alight on a tree or on the ground.

A close view of the red-legged partridge reveals a strikingly handsome bird. The adult has white cheeks bordered with black, red bill and legs, and brightly barred flanks. Its red-brown tail is seen in flight. The scarce little owl also inhabits the fields and farmland of Harkerside (*walk 6*) where it finds a hollow tree or old farm building to

nest in. You may see its diminutive form perched on a wall or post, as it is active by day and feeds mainly on beetles. In winter, sparrowhawks and kestrels frequent the farmland of the dale, when very large flocks of fieldfares and redwings come to feed on the hawthorn and rowan berries and in the stubble fields.

Villages and farm buildings It is exciting to hear the scream of swifts on a summer's evening as they dash across the sky picking up small insects. As dusk approaches they fly higher, spending the night on the wing. Yorkshire flagstone roofs provide just the right size of gap for swifts to enter, where they build a scrappy nest under the roof. Swallows will use a barn or porch, where they build a cup-shaped nest of mud and straw, and the house martin builds a very fine mud nest normally under the eaves of a house. The most colourful of our finches, the goldfinch, is also a common sight near to villages and delightful to watch. Often in groups, known as charms, they feed on thistle heads or seeds of groundsel and their song is a high-pitched liquid twitter. The greenfinch is a little duller but common enough in gardens and on the edge of woods, but a good sighting would be the linnet, the male having red colouring on breast and forehead. In winter, siskins, green woodpecker and tawny owl have been seen feeding in gardens.

To be successful in observing birds, you have to learn to move silently and unobtrusively, to make use of cover such as a wall or tree, and to make no sudden movements. It is a matter of patience and learning by experience. It helps to wear clothing with subdued colours and made of soft, noiseless material. A good birdbook is always worth having with you. The best way is to take along with you a keen and knowledgeable companion, who can help identify birds quickly and accurately.

Mammals Keep an eye open for the unexpected. You may be fortunate to see a mink along the riverbank. The soft, glossy dark brown fur can look almost black, and you may be able to approach near to it. Half as big again as a stoat, the mink measures twenty-one inches (52cm) long, including the tail. It will hunt rabbits and mice as well as catch fish, and water voles are becoming rare because of mink. Stoats are quite common and may be seen chasing a rabbit or other prey. In winter it is not unusual to find one in creamy white ermine, or perhaps still a patchy brown and white, but the tip of the tail will remain black. The smaller weasel is also fairly common. It has no black tip to its tail and lives mainly on mice.

Occasionally a roe deer may be seen. In summer they are red-brown but moult in the autumn to grow a thicker dark brown coat. They are most active at dawn and dusk, and are seen more in the winter months when there is less vegetation and when they are on the move looking for food. Hares can commonly be seen in the fields or on the moors at any time of the year, being bigger than rabbits with long, black-tipped ears. The males and females are known as Jacks and Jills. As regards that elusive and attractive animal, the otter, it is reported that the odd one is still seen in Swaledale, possibly while travelling across country.

At sunset on summer evenings in the villages, the pipistrelle bats are out in profusion. This is the smallest and most common of the dozen or so bats seen in Britain. Its tiny head and body measure less than 1½ inches (35mm) though its wing span is 8½ inches (22cm). Breeding sites are often in the roof space of houses, where it is relatively warm and sheltered.

Fish Small headwater streams have bullhead and brown trout. The latter thrive on the well-oxygenated water as it splashes and plunges along, feeding on insect larvae of mayflies and stoneflies. The Swale has dace, a slim cylindrical fish, olive green on the back and with silvery flanks, the underside fins being yellowish. It grows up to ten inches (25cm). The bottom-feeding barbel can reach twice this length and anglers know it as a fighting fish, though it is not considered edible. Other fish of general occurrence include minnow, gudgeon, three-spined stickleback and eel.

Butterflies and moths These attractive insects like warm, dry weather and plenty of sunshine, so the number of species in Swaledale is limited. The only butterflies breeding higher up the dale are small tortoiseshell, green-veined white, small heath and green hairstreak. The small heath, recognised by its rather dull, pale orange colour, can do quite well in cloudy conditions and is to be found on rough grassland up to the heather moors, whereas the meadow brown requires more sunshine and is only found in the lower part of the dale, near Richmond. South-facing limestone scars can locally act as suntraps and together with the wild flowers attract many butterflies. The ringlet is dark-brown in colour with eyelets which are especially noticeable on the underside when the wings are closed. At a distance it can be confused with the male meadow brown. It is a species that has expanded into the lower dale and it has been suggested that this has been aided by the county council policy of only cutting a metre-wide strip along the grass verges. Others to look out for are the wall butterfly, common blue and large skipper. The peacock butterfly may be seen in the spring, but the main brood are conspicuous in late summer and autumn. Occasional migrating butterflies

Some of the butterflies to be seen in the dale. Top: *ringlet (above and below).* Middle: *small copper and meadow brown.* Bottom: *Small heath.*

from the Continent, such as the red admiral and painted lady, occur at all altitudes. A pair of binoculars can be very useful in identifying butterflies.

If you are on the heather moors, look out for the day-flying moths, northern eggar and fox moth. They are both large, with a two inch (50cm) wing span, and rather similar, being reddish-brown in colour. The northern eggar has small single pale spots on the wings and the fox moth has two bars. They both produce dark brown hairy caterpillars which hibernate in the winter months among the heather roots. An even larger and more striking insect is the emperor moth which is a brownish-grey

with large yellow and blue eye spots on the wings. The male flies by day and can detect the presence of a female at a distance of up to 1,100 yards (1,000m). The fully grown caterpillar is a bright green with yellow spots, definitely a warning to birds seeking a juicy meal. Smaller species of the acid moorland include antler moths, map-winged swifts, twin-spot carpets and chevrons, all of which may be abundant. A good moth book is needed to identify them. There are many more to look out for in other habitats where there is a greater variety of food plants; over 300 species of larger moths having been recorded in the Dales area.

FLORA

The colourful hay meadows of Swaledale are one of its most outstanding features. They are spectacular in June when enriched by a great variety of wild flowers. With a backdrop of drystone walls, stone field barns and the nearby river, the meadows turn first yellow, mainly with buttercups, then white with splashes of purple when pignut and wood cranesbill dominate. On sunny slopes, especially where the soils are rich in lime, grows quite a different group of flowers; and the many small woodlands harbour further delights for the walker to explore, while the broad heather moors, the bogs and springs have their own, often hidden, attractions. Swaledale is noted for its sheer profusion of flowers rather than for its rarities and, because there is very little true lowland habitat and fewer hedgerows, there are fewer species than in the other dales. Even in 1909, the botanist Arnold Lees noted that Swaledale had only 600 species compared to Wensleydale's 700.

Swaledale in the spring brings the smell of wild garlic which pervades the woodlands, and on more open banks, primroses grow in profusion. By early summer you get a wonderful impression of the many colourful wild flowers; but some stand out, ones which you may regard as being perhaps special to the dale – or rather the dale supplies the right habitat for them. Perhaps the most obvious is the blue geranium, known as meadow cranesbill, which in summer lines roadside verges where it mixes with the somewhat paler, tall, blue spikes of giant bellflower. The mountain pansy is widely scattered on pastures and grassland, and shows interesting colour variations. The most common of these pansies are deep yellow, and grow well near Booze (*walk 8*) and other parts of Arkengarthdale. Blue forms and some half-yellow and half-blue appear near Ravenseat 1,300 feet (400m) above sea level (*walk 19*), and others grow near to Keld (*also walk 19*). You may also find the odd flower with the upper pair of petals purple, the middle pair blue and the lower one yellow. Along Shaw Beck (*walk 4*) there are mountain pansies which are cream and yellow.

One flower which is truly characteristic of Swaledale is the melancholy thistle. In July the lovely purple flowerheads on tall stems grow by the roadside and in the hay meadows around Muker (*walks 17 and 18*). This northern plant has long leaves, white on the back, with no prickles, and was first discovered near Ingleborough. It is not

The presence of mountain pansy indicates a leached soil.

really a 'sad' flower, but because of its drooping buds and solitary head was once thought to cure melancholia. The seventeenth century herbalist Culpeper claimed that leaves steeped in wine would 'make a man as merry as a cricket'. No doubt it was the wine that did the trick.

A favourite flower locality is the lower end of Gunnerside Gill, from the village of Gunnerside up to Sir Francis Mine (*walk 14*). There is a good variety of habitats on a mixture of soils, with deciduous woodland, grassy banks, pastures, wet patches and leadmining spoil. One of the interesting plants in April or May is toothwort, which has no chlorophyll and therefore no green pigment. Crowded down one side of the stem, the flowers are creamy coloured with pale pink petals, and it has been called the 'corpse flower' because of its sickly appearance. A parasite on hazel or elm, it is found near the base of these trees where it takes sap directly from the roots. At the same time of year you will see the loosely-flowered spikes of early purple orchid. Another woodland flower, usually a rich purple colour, this orchid smells of tomcats, and its tuberous root looks like a pair of testicles. The Greek herbalist Dioscorides recorded that couples could determine the sex of future children, a boy if the father ate the larger tuber or a girl if the mother ate the smaller one!

Another good spot for flowers is along the river from Stang Bridge to Whaw in Arkengarthdale (*walk 9*). Marsh orchids grow on the grass verge near the road junction and, in the field next to the bridge, white flowers of meadow saxifrage appear on the grassy slopes. The kidney-shaped leaves of meadow saxifrage encircle the base of the flower stem, which is tall and branched near the top. Brooklime (one of the speedwells) and bog stitchwort grow in wet patches, with mountain pansy and ragged robin near the second footbridge.

Some Flower Habitats:

Hay meadows A rarity in Britain are the old-fashioned, flowery hay meadows which are best seen in the Yorkshire Dales. Swaledale has the most, and some of the finest. They are strung out on the deeper soils on both sides of the Swale between Reeth and Muker (*walks 11, 13, 16 and 18*). Much of the farmland here is now an ESA, or Environmentally Sensitive Area, where traditional management is carried out.

In the spring, the meadows are usually grazed by ewes until they have their lambs when, in mid-May, the flocks go up onto the rough grazings. Warmer days and nutrients from the manure help the hay-crop to grow rapidly for two months until it is cut in late July, or in August at higher altitudes or if the weather is poor. Most of the flowers have time to produce seed before then, and they also give the hay an added richness as animal fodder. The flower meadows depend entirely on the traditional way of farming, and if the grass were left uncut and ungrazed, then the fields would soon revert to grass and scrub with fewer flowers.

Although occasionally flooded in the winter, most fields are well-drained during the growing season, and here the delicate white pignut, yellow rattle and the yellow daisy, known as cat's ear, grow well. The wetter corners may support kingcup, bistort and lady's smock. The soils are deep and fertile, being developed from river sediments and glacial deposits, and tend to be mostly neutral. The meadows are often referred to as species-rich, and in his book *Conservation of Northern Meadows* Roger Smith gives the number of species at between twenty and twenty-five in an average square metre.

Flowers in a hay meadow have to compete for light with tall grasses, and so they themselves are tall and strong, often

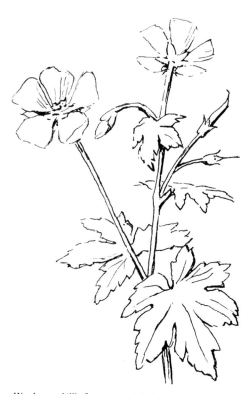

Wood cranesbill's flowers are pinkish-purple.

with a spreading root system. Wood cranesbill has all these features and is frequent in the richest and least improved meadows, known as 'cranesbill meadows'. Such meadows include northern species near the southern extent of their range, such as wood cranesbill itself, the lovely melancholy thistle and the rarer globe-flower. Wood cranesbill has bright pinkish-purple flowers with white centres. Pignut, yellow rattle and knapweed are common, but in damper corners are replaced by common bistort and lady's smock. Other flowers include meadow and bulbous buttercups, and the hawkweeds, cat's ear and rough hawkbit. Typical grasses are sweet vernal-grass, red fescue, Yorkshire fog and crested dogstail.

Lower down the dale, many of the species-rich meadows have been replaced by intensively-managed grass swards. The application of chemical fertilizers, for example, can double the yield of hay per acre, but at the same time reduces the number of flowering species by fifty per cent. If a meadow is completely reseeded with high yielding grasses, then it becomes a dead area as far as bees, butterflies, other insects and seed- and insect-eating birds are concerned, not to mention many small mammals. Research is going on to find out how to restore such 'improved' meadows to their traditional state.

Wet places Around springs and ditches and in the wetter parts of meadows grows a distinctive collection of moisture-loving plants – ragged robin, marsh valerian, brooklime, kingcups, marsh ragwort and marsh orchids. Ragged robin is becoming a rarity in many places, but in Swaledale it is still commonly seen. From the end of June you will see patches of the bright pink flowers near Arkle Beck (*walk 9*) and in Gilling Wood (*walk 2*), where there is also a white variety. Each of the five petals is deeply divided into four narrow strips, giving the plant its ragged appearance. The flowers are often pollinated by green-veined white butterflies.

The alder also likes to have its feet near water. Common along riverbanks and ditches, along Arkle Beck below Whaw (*walk 9*) and the Swale below Gunnerside (*walk 13*), it is easily recognised in winter by the cone-like fruits. Alder roots contain nodules that fix nitrogen from the air (like the pea family), useful in wet soil where this element may be lacking; the roots also help to prevent erosion of the riverbank.

At the head of the dale, in sphagnum bog, you may find cross-leaved heath, the yellow spikes of bog asphodel and marsh violet, and it is worth looking out for the tiny round-leaved sundew, the sticky leaves of which are a reddish colour. Cranberry is a small trailing plant, often over sphagnum. On wet rocks you may see New Zealand willowherb, another trailer with tiny white flowers on the end of long stems (*walks 16 and 17*).

Rough grassland Between improved pastures and the open moorland are broad stretches of rough grassland, for example on the south side of Calver Hill (*walk 10*) and on the flanks of Harkerside (*walk 6*). Rainfall is heavy and soils are almost all acidic. The yellow, four-petalled tormentil and white mats of heath bedstraw are common, and less frequent are heath speedwell, a lovely pale blue flower, heath spotted orchid and mountain pansy.

Calcareous grassland and limestone banks There are only small patches of calcareous grassland and these reflect the underlying rock. The limestone of Tailbridge, on the way up to Nine Standards Rigg (*walk 20*), is a rather special high-altitude example and includes the only limestone pavement in Swaledale. The thin soils support a covering of blue moor-grass, rare in other parts of the country, and flowers such as fairy flax, salad burnet and rockrose.

There are many small limestone outcrops that, on a well-drained slope and perhaps facing the sun, provide a wonderful variety of colour. There is such a bank near Orgate Farm (*walk 4*), another near Downholme Bridge (*walk 5*) and a third in Deepdale (*walk 3*), each with a good diversity of plants. If you see the lemon-yellow daisy of mouse-eared hawkweed, salad burnet or the purple of wild thyme, then you know that limestone is near the surface;

The delicate harebell hangs on a slender stem.

marjoram and rockrose are other lime-loving species.

Woodland Only 1½% of Swaledale is wooded, and consists of many small woodland patches scattered along the length of the dale with a few bigger areas lower down – just remnants of what, a thousand years ago, must have been continuous forest. They are now mainly of ash and sycamore with less frequent birch, rowan and bird cherry. Sycamore is often the most

common tree – oak being rare – while
hawthorn, hazel and holly form the shrub
layer. Beech has sometimes been planted
as, for example, in Scar House Wood (*walk
8*) in Arkengarthdale, and pine and larch
may be found among the broadleaved trees.
Alder and goat willow are grown along
riverbanks to prevent erosion.

Common flowers are dog's mercury,
bluebell and wild garlic, and any of these
can cover wide patches of the woodland
floor. The delicate wood sorrel, herb
robert, wood avens and enchanter's night-
shade are also frequent species. Birbeck
Wood in Gunnerside Gill (*walk 14*) and
Rowleth Wood (*walk 13*) are both ancient
woodlands and contain some interesting
species, including violets, primroses and
early purple orchid. Plantations of spruce
and pine occur here and there (*walk 2*), and
a few with broad-leaved shelterbelts have
been recently planted, as on Richmond Out
Moor (*walk 2*).

Heather moors The extensive moors on
each side and at the head of Swaledale
(*walks 12, 15 and 20*) cover a surprisingly
large area. They have developed on the
high, gently sloping upland of gritstones
and shales of the Millstone Grit series.
Rainfall is heavy and drainage poor, which
has resulted in the formation of a blanket
bog, where peat is actively accumulating.
The natural vegetation over a large part of
these moors is heather (or ling) which in
August turns a glorious purple. The
heather is carefully managed by the estates
to further the interests and numbers of the
red grouse population. Years of management by burning, grazing and drainage may
have extended the area of heather, though
recent research suggests that intensive
sheep-grazing is causing heather to retreat
from the areas of drier heath.

Harestail cotton grass, which grows in
tussocks, also covers large parts of the moor

Ragged robin favours wet places.

and often grows with the heather in a cotton grass/heather mixture. Other plants of the high, wet moors are bilberry (often around rocky outcrops), cowberry, a related plant with pinkish-white flowers and red berries, purple moor-grass and bog mosses (of the sphagnum type). Cloudberry is a kind of high altitude bramble with large white flowers and orange fruit; its broad green leaves are conspicuous among the dark stems of the heather.

Leadmining spoil It is not surprising that leadmining spoil covers a greater area in Swaledale than in any other dale, and it is most extensive on the north side of the dale and between Swaledale and Arkengarth-dale. Spoil is made up of coarse gritty sand, gravel and broken rock and is often only sparsely covered by vegetation, but the plants which do survive this rather sterile habitat are unique and of great botanical interest.

Cushions of spring sandwort, with their starry white flowers, are commonly found around the spoil heaps. This plant prefers a small amount of lead in its diet, as does another plant, alpine pennycress, only found near to old leadmines; sheep's sorrel is also lead-tolerant. Where the soils are less toxic, wild thyme grows, and on the valley floors such as near Francis Mine in Gunnerside Gill (*walk 14*) and along Shaw Beck (*walk 4*), spring sandwort and mountain pansies grow together in more neutral soils.

Other Interesting Plants:

Fungi Mushrooms and toadstools are more common in woods than on grassland, and autumn is the best time to see them. An attractive and interesting group, they are worth getting to know as they make a fascinating study. Distinctive ones include the bracket fungus, which juts out of the

The stinkhorn smells of rotting flesh.

trunks of trees in spectacular fashion. The shaggy inkcap is a gill toadstool with an elongated cap which opens to become an attractive conical shape. The gills then turn into a black, inky liquid. Boletes (pronounced *boh-leets*) are a group of large toadstools which, instead of gills, have small tubes containing the spores and give the underside of the cap a spongy texture.

One that you can smell before you spot it is the stinkhorn (*walk 2*); the putrid and penetrating smell attracts flies to aid dispersal of spores. The common stinkhorn begins as an egg shape, about three inches (8cm) across, splits and within a few hours a white spongy stalk with a green head pushes up to a height of six inches (15cm) or so. The puffball is another species which, when ripe, will give off its spores in a puff of 'smoke' at the slightest disturbance, as when hit by a raindrop. Many fungi are edible and a few are poisonous, so the aspiring gourmet must be quite sure of identifying them correctly – an accurate book is an essential guide.

Ferns Brittle bladder fern occurs widely on limestone walls and rocks. The pretty fronds are slender and fragile, about a foot (30cm) long with a stalk. Maidenhair spleenwort is a beautiful little fern with a shiny black stem which grows on limestone cliffs and screes (*walk 17*). Its rarer cousin, green spleenwort, is entirely green and grows in similar places. Wall rue looks less like a fern with its irregular leafy appearance and is common on walls (*walk 2*). Check by looking at the underside of the leaflets to see the spore-producing sacs.

Horsetails Today there is only one group of horsetails, *Equisetum*, but they were important plants in the great coal forests of Carboniferous times when there were tree-sized species. Giant horsetail grows in lower Swaledale and is unmistakable by its large size. It prefers damp, basic soils on shady slopes and its whitish infertile stems will grow four or five feet high (1.5m). Spores are produced in a cone structure at the tips of some of the stems.

Branched wood horsetail is an occasional rarity on acid soils, particularly in Arkengarthdale but also near Gunnerside (*walk 15*). Its feathery appearance is most attractive, each delicate drooping branch being itself branched.

Insect-eating plants There are two fascinating plants which prey on insects. They are both found in wet boggy areas where soils are poor and, because of the lack of nutrients, cleverly supplement their diet by extracting mineral salts such as nitrates and phosphates from captured flies and other small insects. Butterwort is fairly common and easily recognised, its yellow-green rosette of leaves sending up slender stems with attractive, trumpet-shaped purple flowers. They are also known as bog violets. When a fly lands on the sticky leaf and begins to struggle, the edges of the leaf curl round the victim and secrete digestive juices which break down the soft parts of the insect. Round-leaved sundew behaves in a similar way, being particularly attractive to midges, and it has been estimated that one sundew plant can catch 2,000 small insects in one season. In Swaledale it is rarer than butterwort and occurs in Gunnerside Gill (*walk 14*) and on Nine Standards Rigg (*walk 20*).

WALK 1: RICHMOND AND EASBY ABBEY

Start: Richmond Market Place. Grid Ref: 171 009
Distance: 3½ miles (5½km)
OS Maps: Pathfinder 609 or Landranger 92
Walking Time: a leisurely two hours

The centre of Richmond is the starting place for this historically interesting short stroll. First along the banks of the River Swale, the walk visits the picturesque ruins of Easby Abbey, then Easby parish church where there are thirteenth century wall paintings. The return is made across the old railway bridge and along the track of the railway line to Station Bridge. The largest car park in Richmond is off Victoria Road, a few minutes walk from the market place.

Richmond is a beautiful and romantic little town in a wonderful position at the entrance to Swaledale. It was the *riche mont* or 'strong hill' of the Norman lords, of Count Alan, who was given the 199 manors of Richmondshire for his hand in keeping the English down in the dreadful Harrying of the North. A fine defensive site was chosen on top of a steep limestone rock which rises high above the Swale, and is

The Swale at Richmond, with its bridge and castle.

crowned by impregnable walls that no army has ever dared attack. A massive 100 foot (30m) high keep is the focus of one of the earliest stone castles in England. A new walled town was planned and laid out, which still retains its Continental style with wide cobbled market place and shops and inns looking on. In the middle of the square is Holy Trinity Church, which once had shops in its aisles, and is now a museum of the Green Howards.

Richmond has a wealth of history, has been immortalised by the painter Turner and is renowned for the song *The Lass of Richmond Hill*. Time has been kind to it, beautiful scenery surrounds it and the town has inspired many visitors. It is a fascinating place to wander round, and full of surprises.

To start the walk to Easby, leave the market place at the top corner by the Richmond Hotel and, after a few paces down New Road, bear left down the cobbled, narrow way of Cornforth Hill. The arch of the Bar is a gateway in the wall of the town, and was built about 1312 for access to the market place and to keep out Scottish raiders. It now forms a picturesque corner on a street so steep it has a handrail. Join Bridge Street and go down past the Green where, on the corner, a house dated 1689 has two sundials, one facing south-west and the other south-east.

Turn left along the bank of the river below the castle walls. There is a legend that, deep below Richmond Castle, King Arthur and his knights lie sleeping until England needs them again. The sword Excalibur must be drawn and the horn sounded in order to wake them and save the country. A simple man of the town, Potter Thompson, discovered the very cave under the castle where he saw the knights and King Arthur. He tried to draw the sword but lost his nerve. The sleepers woke and, as he fled, a mocking cry came to his ears:

'If thou hadst either drawn the sword, or blown the horn,
Thou'd been the luckiest man that ever yet was born!'

The Swale here runs in a gorge, over bedrock and on to the falls, where the river drops over rock steps in an attractive setting and the valley opens out again. At this point a plaque reminds passers-by that here was the Richmond gasworks, one of the first public gas suppliers in Europe.

The path continues through the park, known as the Batts. On the hillside is the school where Charles Dodgson was a pupil and who later wrote under his famous pseudonym, Lewis Carroll. One of his early poems was published in the school magazine. Straight ahead is Station Bridge, built in 1847 to link the new railway station with the town.

Keeping to the riverside, go under the bridge, then left and right to where a sign says 'Easby Abbey ¼' and where a lovely garden spreads up the hillside. The peaceful woodland track leads past limestone springs and between lofty beeches. At a fork in the path you can take either route, but if you keep near the riverbank, there are some fine big lime trees and a variety of flowers beneath them. Not far to the left of this footpath (*see map*) is a remnant of Scots Dyke, an ancient wall or embankment, many miles in length, that may have been the boundary of a Celtic kingdom. Step up into a field, where the river is eroding away its bank, to reach the abbey.

Here on a bend in the river, in a delightful situation, are the attractive and extensive ruins of Easby Abbey, dating from 1152. The layout is unusual and there are still a few well-preserved buildings. The dining hall has some beautiful windows and a reader's pulpit, from which the white canons (of the Premonstratensian order) listened to readings during the meal. The

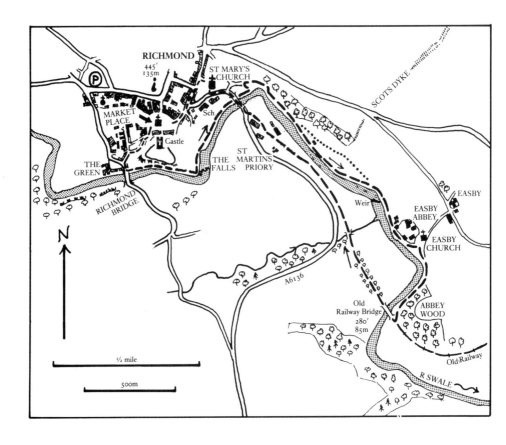

RICHMOND
445'
135m
ST MARY'S
CHURCH
MARKET
PLACE
Sch
Castle
THE
GREEN
ST
THE MARTINS
FALLS PRIORY
RICHMOND
BRIDGE
SCOTS DYKE
EASBY
Weir
EASBY
ABBEY
EASBY
CHURCH
N
A6136
Old
Railway Bridge
280'
85m
ABBEY
WOOD
Old Railway
R SWALE
½ mile
500m

guest rooms and latrines, the large building nearest to the river, occupied three storeys. The gatehouse, which lies on the other side of the parish church, has survived well and only lacks a roof.

It was a large and apparently prosperous abbey, though it did suffer from the Scottish raids. On one occasion in 1346, the English army was billeted there and the drunken brawling of the troops caused as much damage as the Scots may have done! At the Dissolution the bell and stalls went to the church of St Mary, Richmond, and a fine carved oak screen to Wensley Church.

Next to the abbey is Easby Church and, like the abbey, was dedicated to St Agatha of Sicily. It was in existence some time before the abbey and was restored by the Scrope, Aske and Conyers families in 1423. A beautifully-carved stone cross from about AD 700 may have marked the site. The stones of the cross were built into the church and only discovered in the twentieth century. A copy now stands on the north side of the chancel. The font is Norman and one of the oldest in the country. The lively and extensive thirteenth century wall paintings tell stories from the Bible and must have given the church a bright and attractive interior for poor people who could not read, or had no pictures of their own.

36

The ruins of Easby Abbey: the guest rooms and latrines.

Continue the walk along the lane past the abbey car park and through two white gates. Turn right over the former railway bridge and view the Swale from above. The rocks on the riverbed have a chequered joint pattern as if paved by man. From the path along the old railway line there are wonderful views of the abbey across the river, and on both sides of the track grow a great assortment of wild roses, elderberry, hawthorn, silver birch and blackberries, and many interesting flowers.

Towards the end of the cinder track and before the first of the old railway buildings, on farmland to the left, are the ruins of St Martins Priory. A Norman doorway is probably the oldest part, and a square tower stands out which may have been a porter's lodge. However, the remains have been used as a source of stone for building and not much is left. This Benedictine found-ation was built soon after the Conquest by the wealthy parent abbey of St Marys in York, and is the oldest building in the dale. At the Dissolution it had a prior and nine monks.

Pass Richmond's modern swimming pool and go up the steps between the former station buildings, which now include a garden centre, and on to the road and Station Bridge. The stone bridge is a fine example of Victorian railway architecture, and from it there is a wonderful view of Richmond Castle and the Swale, much as Turner saw it in 1817.

Cross the bridge towards the town and, halfway up the hill, call in to see another old church, that of St Mary, known to have been in existence by 1135, though only the fine fifteenth century tower survived the Victorian restoration. The magnificent stalls are from Easby Abbey, there is an elaborate monument to Sir Timothy Hutton and his family, and some fine woodwork by the 'mouse man' Robert Thompson of Kilburn. In the churchyard you can see the plague stone and the tombstone of Robert Willance, the man who survived a leap over Whitcliffe Scar (*see walk 3*). If you leave the churchyard by Church Wynd you can see something of the fine Georgian town houses in Frenchgate. At the top of Frenchgate is Hill House, now rather shrouded by trees and bushes, where Frances I'Anson, the 'Lass of Richmond Hill', stayed on occasions. It was her mother's old home and used as a holiday retreat. The verse was written by Leonard McNally who eventually married the 'sweet lass'. Turn left to reach the market place and starting point.

WALK 2: GILLING WEST AND HARTFORTH

Start: Richmond, tourist information centre. Grid Ref: 171 010
Distance: 9½ miles (15km)
OS Maps: Pathfinder 609 or Landranger 92
Walking Time: 5 hours

This is one of the longer walks in this collection, but it is not very strenuous. It passes Aske Hall, continues through wheat fields and pastures to Gilling West and Hartforth. Then it climbs up along the ancient Jagger Lane through the pine woods and open moors to reach a height of 960 feet (293m) above sea level, before a gentle downhill finish over Richmond's old racecourse.

Just across from Richmond's information centre and bordering Friars Wynd is the delightful Georgian Theatre Royal, together with its own museum. It is the most complete eighteenth century theatre in existence, built by actor-manager Samuel Butler and was opened on the 2nd September 1788. It fell into disuse after 1840 and it wasn't until a hundred years later that interest was focused on it and restoration began. It re-opened in 1963, and the best way to experience the intimate atmosphere of this amazing little theatre is to attend one of the regular performances.

Start the walk along Queens Road and by the tall tower of Greyfriars. In its glorious early days, Richmond must have been filled with all kinds of religious people: white canons, black nuns and white nuns, friars in grey, priests and monks. The friars, followers of St Francis of Assisi, wore grey and followed a life of poverty, working among the people. The late fifteenth century Greyfriars Tower was a sign of growing materialism in the order and is all that remains of the Franciscan friary, founded in 1258.

Continue up Queens Road to the corner of Quakers Lane and take the narrow footpath straight ahead, up a ginnel between houses. At the top, on Green Howards Road, turn right, then left along another narrow path to the rear of some

houses and across a sports field. At the far right corner of the field, follow the signs for Richmond golf club. Pass in front of the clubhouse. (Be alert for flying golfballs!) Exit from the golf course through a group of sycamores and turn right for 220 yards (200m) along the edge of Low Wood. The crop of wheat, though fairly clean of weeds, still has a few red poppies and the pineapple weed underfoot really does smell of pineapple.

Go left over the stile and straight through the wood, crossing the track. In summer there are all kinds of flowers in the wood: foxglove, figwort and yellow pimpernel, and near the wooden footbridge over Aske Beck, richly-scented meadowsweet, the rose-red flowers of greater willowherb and the delightful pink of ragged robin.

Cross the parkland past fine oaks, beeches, horse chestnuts and grazing Jacob sheep, to the front of Aske Hall. The Askes had lived here for 500 years when, in 1536, Robert Aske became commander of the Pilgrimage of Grace. He led 30,000 pilgrims into York then Hull and eventually to Pontefract, where he was promised a redress by the king. But events went the other way and, in July 1537 on a market day in York, Robert Aske was publically hanged on top of Clifford Tower. By 1600, Aske Hall was in the possession of the Whartons and it later went to Sir Lawrence Dundas,

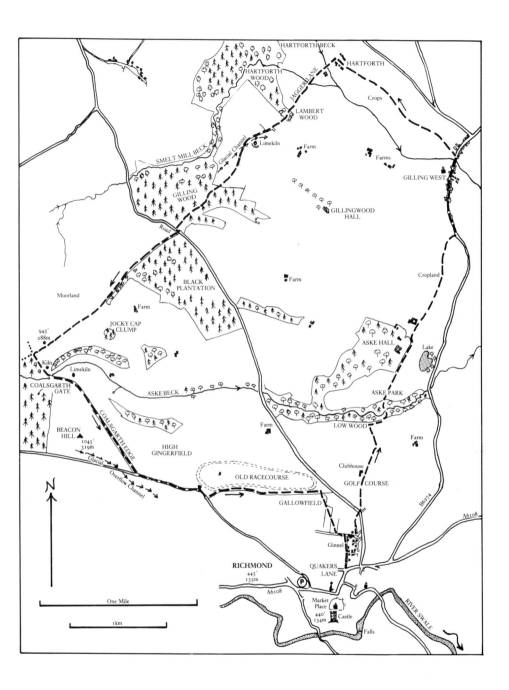

whose descendant was made Earl of Zetland in 1838.

There is a view of the stately mansion to the left, beyond a good collection of exotic trees, and the fern, wall rue, decorates the balustrade. In 1818, Thomas Dundas, Earl of Zetland, became MP for Richmond when he was only twenty-three. He was a popular benefactor of schools and churches in the district, and bred racehorses, including a winner of the Derby. Turner painted the *View of Aske Hall, the Seat of Lord Dundas* in 1817. Over to the right, in a picturesque setting, a small lake is home for swans, nesting coots, mallard and tufted duck.

Pass a line of limes to leave the driveway by a stile on the left and through the fields to Gilling. An old quarry shelters hawthorn, elderberry and the musk thistle, the latter being distinguished from spear thistle by its large, purple nodding head. Listen for the drumming of the great spotted woodpecker and the *chiz-iz-iz-iz-iz-zeee* of the yellowhammer on this part of the walk.

Turn left along the road into Gilling West. A roadside seat declares 'best kept village 1973' and there is an attractive main street with stone cottages and two pubs, but Gilling has seen greater times. It was the headquarters of the Anglian kings of Deira, where the Earls of Mercia ruled and where the kings of Northumbria came to relax at their country seat. It was second only to York in importance. The historian Bede tells of the tragic murder of the humble and pious Oswin, seventh century king of Deira, which is thought to have occurred here in Gilling.

Go over the stone bridge and turn left through the fields to Hartforth, ignoring the path to the right. Crops include potatoes, rapeseed, wheat and barley. Go through the white gate by the collection of houses which make up Hartforth and view

Heron are most active at dawn and dusk.

the hall through the trees ahead. In the 1680s the hamlet was the home of Philip Swale, Quaker, landowner and leadminer, and attorney to Lord Wharton.

Turn left onto the old packhorse route of Jagger Lane, which here is no more than a footpath. Heron may be seen along here, either along the small streams or by a pond on the left; the sparrowhawk also frequents the area. The two streams are crossed by footbridges, the first across Hartforth Beck, an ornamental stone one with parapets of stone pillars. The second footbridge over Smelt Mill Beck appears to replace a former packhorse bridge, and from here a sunken section of Jagger Lane leads up the side of a field. A jagger was a man in charge of a packhorse train, and ponies loaded with lead from Swaledale must have passed along here on their way north. The train may have consisted of some thirty ponies and the jagger would have had one or two men to help him. The leading pony had a bell to warn travellers or other packhorse trains. Constant use of the track eroded it, so that it often ran in a deep hollow. When it became too wet and deep in mud, another parallel track would be used.

The sunken lane enters a small wood and becomes wet underfoot. Some of the trees of oak, hazel and sycamore have their boughs draped with honeysuckle which in summer gives off a sweet perfume. Honeysuckle's other name is woodbine, as the plant coils itself tightly round young trees. Keep straight on (there are paths to left and right) and head up the slope to the gate into Gilling Wood. The wide stony track climbs further up the hill. The trees are pines and larches, but there is some interesting ground flora. At the lower end of the wood, a disgusting smell may reach your nostrils. Look around for stinkhorn, a fast-growing fungus. It grows out of a white egg to six or eight inches (15-20cm) with a green slimy head. Flies are attracted to it and eat it, helping to disperse the spores. The phallic shape led the publishers of *Gerard's Herbal* in 1633 to print the illustration upside down, so as not to offend readers. Other flowers along the trackside include yellow pimpernel, the bright blue flowers of brooklime, pink and white varieties of ragged robin and tall foxgloves.

Turn left at the road, then right to continue along a wide stony track. To the

Honeysuckle brings fragrance to a wood.

right is a broad view towards Ravensworth and to the left is a conifer plantation. As the path passes the tree-capped Jockey Cap Hill, on the left, and reaches its highest point, the packhorse route continues along the edge of heathland. Linnets sing from scattered gorse bushes and curlews call across the moor.

Turn left along the wall, with a young plantation on the right where a band of deciduous trees has been planted. On the left is a double limekiln and near here you may see small heath and ringlet butterflies. Even up here at 900 feet (275m) above sea level, the ringlet seems to be extending its range, right into the hills. This attractive butterfly is a dark brown with a string of false eyes on the underside. It has a life span of two weeks in July and will even fly in the rain. The female lays her eggs in flight, dropping them onto common grasses, which the caterpillars will feed on in the autumn to become fully grown the following spring.

At Coalsgarth Gate, ford the stream and keep the wall on the left. It leads onto a lane with a distant view over Coalsgarth Edge, the Vale of Mowbray and the Cleveland Hills; to the right is Beacon Hill. On reaching the road, turn left past Gingerfield Lodge, and off the road to the left, after the cottages, and on to Low Moor. Gingerfield is one of the old 'fields' of medieval Richmond, the others being Westfield, Gallowfield, Eastfield and Whitfield.

The path passes a stone tower and stays near to the wall on the right. Here is Richmond's old racecourse, still in use for exercising racehorses from local stables. On the crown of the hill is the ruin of the old grandstand. Built in 1775, it had two storeys with an iron balcony, from which many a Gold Cup was followed by the gentry of the day. In the summer months, wild flowers and butterflies abound along these south-facing slopes; among them are meadow vetchling and meadow cranesbill, hoary plantain and black medick.

The meadow brown is the most common butterfly in Britain. The male is smaller and much darker than the female, and closer in colour to the ringlet. Both may be found here in July. You may also find two orange-brown butterflies, the solid-looking large skipper with a wingspan of just under an inch and a half (35mm), and the brightly-coloured wall brown, wingspan two inches (50mm). The common blue, whose food plants include clover, black medick and birdsfoot trefoil, is also found here. Although the male is blue, the female is brown, and both have white margins round the wings.

Take the second footpath on the right, diagonally across three fields (the ancient Gallowfield) to Green Howards Road. Turn left then, rejoining the first part of the walk, right down the narrow snicket to Quakers Lane and Richmond centre.

WALK 3: DEEPDALE AND WHITCLIFFE SCAR FROM RICHMOND

Start: Richmond Market Place. Grid Ref: 171 009
Distance: 7½ miles (12km)
OS Maps: Pathfinder 609 or Landranger 92
Walking Time: 4 hours

Here is a beautiful and scenic part of lower Swaledale. From Richmond, the walk follows the wooded riverbank to Round Howe, where it continues on the other side of the Swale to Applegarth. A modest climb out of the valley explores Deepdale, Whitcliffe Scar and Willance's Leap. There is a good variety of wild flowers, panoramic views of the dale and an easy return to the town.

Richmond Castle, rising high above the market place, has a grandeur and nobility that makes it one of Yorkshire's finest. The towering keep, the plan of the cobbled market place and the narrow streets, which lead off it, are part of Richmond's 900 year history, but much of the town architecture is Georgian. The great variety of buildings and the fine houses of Frenchgate and Newbiggin tell of the importance of the town in the seventeenth century, and today provide it with a unique character. If you have time, explore Castle Walk high above the river and, for a more extensive panorama and bird's-eye view of the town, try the top of the castle keep.

Begin the walk from the top corner of the market square by the Richmond Hotel and go down the narrow Cornforth Hill, under the old arch of the Bar, a fourteenth century gate to the town. There is a view from here of Culloden Tower on the hill. It was built by an eccentric to commemorate the victory of the English over the Scots at Culloden in 1746. The tall stone tower is octagonal with pointed windows, and Peter Gunn describes it as early Gothic Revival and 'unique in revealing the imaginative charm of eighteenth century England'. Continue steeply down past the Green to Richmond Bridge. The bridge which Leland mentioned had four arches and was shown on a map of 1610. However, this was swept away in the great flood of 1771 and replaced by the present one, designed by John Carr in 1789 with three arches and semicircular cutwaters.

Cross the bridge and, turning right, take the riverside footpath on the far bank. The

A corner of Richmond, with Culloden Tower on the hillside.

43

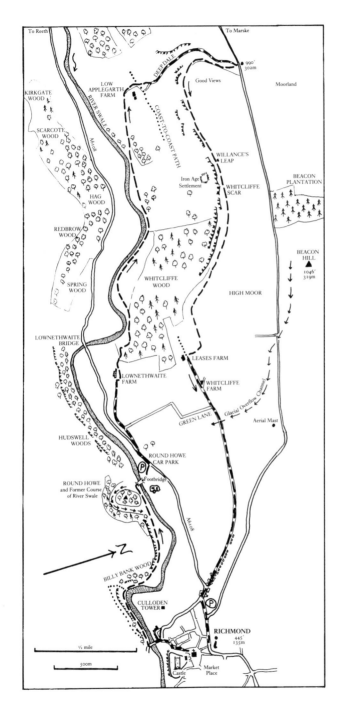

To Reeth

To Marske

990'
302m

Moorland

Good Views

DEEP DALE

LOW
APPLEGARTH
FARM

KIRKGATE
WOOD

COAST-TO-COAST PATH

RIVER SWALE

SCARCOTE
WOOD

Swale

WILLANCE'S
LEAP

BEACON
PLANTATION

Iron Age
Settlement

WHITCLIFFE
SCAR

HAG
WOOD

REDBROW
WOOD

BEACON
HILL
1046'
319m

WHITCLIFFE
WOOD

SPRING
WOOD

HIGH MOOR

LOWNETHWAITE
BRIDGE

LEASES FARM

LOWNETHWAITE
FARM

WHITCLIFFE
FARM

Glacial Overflow Channel

HUDSWELL
WOODS

GREEN LANE

Aerial Mast

ROUND HOWE
CAR PARK

Footbridge

ROUND HOWE
and Former Course
of River Swale

Swale

N

BILLY BANK WOOD

CULLODEN
TOWER

RICHMOND
445'
135m

½ mile

500m

Castle

Market
Place

44

view back of bridge and castle is a classic, a frequent subject for artists and photographers. Walk along the river edge, once a paved path for miners and now much eroded. Take care as the rocks can be slippery. Some enormous slabs of dark limestone were used in making the path, and one piece lying on the bank is covered with small fossil lamp shells (brachiopods), while herb robert and herb bennet grow round about.

If the river is full, you can take a higher path through Billy Bank Wood and rejoin the riverside down some steps, a third of a mile (530m) further on, where the river turns a sharp bend. Not far beyond this point and facing the river is the gated entrance to a copper mine, and tell-tale pieces of rock with streaks of the green copper minerals malachite and chrysocolla can still be found along the path. The mine was worked for low quality ore between 1906 and 1915. A second entrance, now collapsed, is situated just before the wooden stile. The angle of the river is where it is crossed by the Richmond Fault, along which the copper ore forms a mineral vein.

The walk continues across grazing land and along the foot of a wooded scar. On approaching the river again a deep dry valley curves round on the left. This is an abandoned loop of the Swale where the river cut a deep gorge, only to be plugged with glacial material, forcing the river to take its present course. The wooded knoll of Round Howe stands in isolation between the two valleys, having a similar origin to Kisdon Hill in the upper dale. The woods are Hudswell Woods owned by the National Trust.

On reaching the footbridge, cross over to Round Howe car park. Continue straight ahead up the slip road and make a left turn on the A6108. After a few yards at the end of the footway, bear right along the lane.

Among the summer laneside blooms are three 'meadow' flowers: the yellow-flowering and rather straggly meadow vetchling; the large, blue geranium flowers of meadow cranesbill; and the rich-scented, creamy meadowsweet.

The path diverts to the right round Lownethwaite Farm, and enters the lower part of Whitcliffe Wood on a track where the clear, repeated calls of the song thrush echo through the trees and squirrels forage for seeds and nuts. Then, leaving the wood for grazing land and the riverbank, you may disturb a heron or hear the *weet* of a redstart. This is a delightful stretch of river lined with alders, with more of them along a ditch full of waterplants. Over on the left side of the valley is Hag Wood, and up to the right is Whitcliffe Scar. By the fence, which has to be scaled, is a fine wych elm. The leaves have a longer point at the tip than the English elm and the flowers, which appear before the leaves, are purple.

Climb up through fields past a ruined barn to a gate gap below Low Applegarth. Pass a lone elm (another that has not succumbed to Dutch elm disease) and turn up the hill to the right, following the yellow arrows across the Coast-to-Coast footpath, to a stile in the wall. On the far side of the wall there is a narrow tarred road which leads up Deepdale and, on the right, a flowery bank on limestone with an interesting variety of flowers, worth a closer look; heath speedwell is a delicate lilac colour in contrast to the deep blue of germander speedwell; black medick is like a miniature yellow clover, from which it can be distinguished by a tiny tooth at the end of the leaf (hold it against the sky); and dovesfoot cranesbill has small bright purplish-pink flowers with soft downy leaves. Some of these flowers are so small that a lens is useful to pick out detail.

Walk up the private road of the dry valley of Deepdale. This striking ravine is a major glacial drainage channel and was eroded by surging meltwater as it headed for the Swale. On the right is a scenic limestone scar carrying attractive pinnacles and a few clinging yews, and in the short turf near the road you may find rings of the buff-coloured fairy ring toadstool.

At the top of Deepdale there is a gate onto a moorland road. Before the gate turn an acute right, doubling back off the road, to start the high level return route. There are good views up Swaledale and, as the path curves to the left, superb views down the dale too. This is the beginning of Whitcliffe Scar, where a high terrace of the Main limestone drops steeply away to the valley below, making an ideal way for a footpath, though it has proved dangerous at least once in history where the memorial identifies Willance's Leap.

Robert Willance was a draper in Richmond and the son of a wealthy leadmine owner. In 1606, when out hunting, he galloped his horse over the edge of the scar. The horse was killed, and Willance escaped with a broken leg which had to be amputated. The leg was buried in the graveyard, to be joined by the rest of the man at the appropriate time. The tombstone can still be seen in St Marys churchyard. Willance was so amazed and pleased at his survival that he erected three stones dated 1606 where the horse had taken three great leaps. The most recent stone was erected in 1906, to commemorate 300 years since the event.

Just beyond and below Willance's Leap on the right is the most complete Iron Age site in Swaledale. Its excavation revealed two or three cattle enclosures against the cliff, protected by a high rampart to the south. The remains of a two-roomed dwelling lie at the entrance to one of the enclosures. It is thought to have been occupied up to AD 600, well after the Romans had left Britain.

The ring ouzel is distinguished by its white chest bar.

Along the edge of the scar, among the blackthorn, wild roses and brambles, grow limestone bedstraw and wild thyme, rockrose and woodsage. In July the lovely purple spikes of viper's bugloss adorn the steep slope. This plant is said to have been a cure for snake bites (hence the name) from the time of Dioscorides, the herbalist of ancient Greece. Over to the left is the trig point of Beacon Hill, at 1,047 feet (319m) the highest point from here to the North Sea. In former times the signal fire was lit to warn of an invasion.

The path leaves the scar, the keep of Richmond Castle comes into view and the route veers left of a wood, through a gap in the fence. It continues along a line of stunted trees and down to Leases Farm and a lane. Turn left along the lane and on down the road to Richmond. Just beyond Green Lane (a track leading to Round Howe), a dip in the road and a tree-lined gully mark the lower end of a glacial overflow channel which comes from the direction of Beacon Hill. The gully was scoured by meltwater flowing above the Swaledale glacier.

While still amid farmland, listen, at any time of year, for the yellowhammer's high-pitched *little bit of bread and no cheeeeese*. The male has a bright yellow head and breast and is a lusty singer. At the bottom of Westfields, a plaque on the wall tells us that this spot was on the centre line of totality during the solar eclipse of June 1927. Join the main road and follow it to the left, to the town centre.

WALK 4: MARSKE, HELWITH AND SKELTON MOOR

Start: The bridge at Marske. Grid Ref: 104 004
Distance: 7 miles (11 km)
OS Maps: Outdoor Leisure 30 or Landranger 92
Walking Time: 3½ hours

The walk explores the peaceful valleys of Marske Beck and Shaw Beck. There is a variety of habitats for birds, beginning with Clints Wood, and some interesting leadmining remains. The return is over heather-covered Skelton Moor to Skelton and Pillimire packhorse bridge. There is space for a few cars near Marske Bridge.

Marske Bridge must be the oldest bridge in Swaledale. From the beckside, five chamfered ribs of the single arch can be seen, like those on Kilgram Bridge in Wensleydale, and probably date from the fifteenth century. In 1588, £25 was spent on it, and in more modern times it has been widened. The sleepy little village of Marske once had an inn appropriately called the Dormouse and, before the new road was built on the other side of the Swale, was on the main road from Richmond to Reeth. In 1665, George Mason returned from London where the plague was raging. To prevent its spread, six men of Marske were ordered to watch the Masons' house for forty days and nights to ensure that neither he nor his family left to mingle with other people in the village. Today, the neat and attractive village is set in idyllic surroundings, backed by wooded hills with Marske Beck at its foot.

Across the beck is Marske Hall, now private apartments and once the home of the Hutton family. It was built in the 1750s by John Carr of York in the classical symmetrical style. For over 300 years the Hutton family had a substantial influence on the village and the local area. In 1594, Matthew Hutton became Archbishop of York, and it was he who established the estate in Marske. Another Matthew Hutton became Archbishop of Canterbury in 1757.

Many trees were planted over 150 years ago by John Hutton, both in the hall gardens, which reach across the road and down to the river, and in the surrounding countryside. His enthusiasm for farming led him to reclaim some of the nearby moorland. In the well-kept gardens by the river are some interesting exotic birds, including black swans.

Marske Hall is the headquarters of the Swaledale Rescue Organisation, formed in 1966. It provides an important service for visitors and covers a wide area in the north-east part of the National Park. The road to Reeth, up the hill at the back of the hall, is known as 'Hardstiles', and other names along the way of 'Heart Sighs' and 'Cordilleras' reflect the difficulties met by the jaggers and packhorse trains as they made their way to Richmond up and down the steep gradients.

From the bridge, walk up to the church, either through the churchyard or round by the road. Of the original Norman church, only the south door remains. In the seventeenth century it was crudely rebuilt on simple lines after being in a bad state of repair.

From the church, take the field path to the upper end of the village, then left along a wide track and lane. Standing out in the landscape to the left is the stone obelisk and monument to Captain Matthew Hutton of

48

Macclesfield who died in 1814. He had owned a racing stable nearby and wanted to be buried where he could hear the tramping of the racehorses. Ahead is the quiet valley of Marske Beck.

Pass the Methodist church and cottages of Clints, a small hamlet set against high wooded cliffs and which once had its own manor house. Clints Wood, mainly deciduous with ash and sycamore, is a good spot for woodland birds, and besides residents such as the wren, dunnock and chaffinch, you shouldn't have difficulty in seeing, or at least hearing, the chiffchaff or the blackcap. The latter's black crown is its most distinguishing feature. The blackcap nests here in the wood where, in the undergrowth of bushes and brambles, it may be seen flitting among the stems and branches for insects and caterpillars. Its variable and rich song is delivered from dense cover. The chiffchaff is an early arrival and may be heard from late March, its repeated notes coming from a high perch.

On leaving the wood, you get a view of the magnificent Clints Scar up to the right, dotted with pines and yews, and the secluded valley below to the left. Before reaching Orgate Farm there is a good flowery bank on limestone where, in summer, purple mats of wild thyme grow, along with yellow dots of black medick (of the clover family) and the bright yellow flowers of rockrose. The hummocky landscape is a reminder that the Orgate lead vein was mined below here long ago.

The path continues on grass below Orgate Farm, all that remains of a very old settlement. Near the beck are the sites of two smelt mills, and below the bridge is the site of a third smelt mill which was in use until about 1800. In the beck among the trees is Orgate Force, to which a visit may be made by going down the farm track and along the far side of the beck. (If you visit the falls, you can continue the walk on the

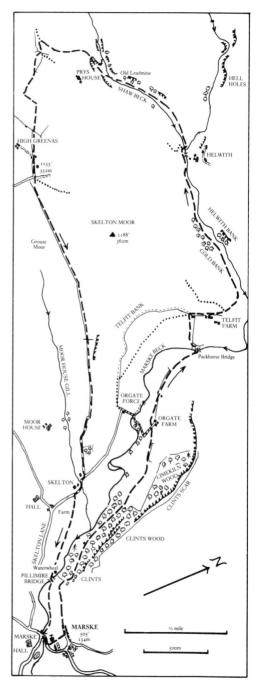

other side of the valley to join the route again at Telfit Farm – *see map*.)

Beyond Orgate Farm, go through the wooden gate and between two barns. Follow the wall (on the left) and gradually drop down before some leadmine tip heaps to cross the beck by a beautifully-built packhorse bridge with a graceful, semi-circular arch, constructed to serve the mines. In the stream are some fine slabs of ripple-marked sandstone. About 220 yards (200m) downstream is the site of the oldest smelt mill in the area, in use in 1589. Cross the bridge where the path leads up to a metal gate on the left of a barn. Turn right onto the track, bear left up the hill, then leave the track where it doubles back, keeping the same direction, and pass through a gate gap and down the hillside to follow Marske Beck further upstream. The view across the beck is north into Throstle Gill.

This is a lovely enclosed valley: jackdaws seem to abound, the kestrel may be seen along the scars, and in the beck are goosander and grey wagtail. Alders grow by a powerful spring on the trackside and, a few paces further on, a wych elm, with purple flowers in April, stands by an out-crop of sandstone. The scattered trees attract redstart, spotted flycatcher and willow warbler. The spotted flycatcher often takes up a perch, where it can easily be seen and from where it can watch for flying insects. This little bird, the size of a robin, with a large, beady black eye and only faint spots on its breast, arrives in May from south of the Sahara. It can be identified best by its behaviour: it has rather an upright stance and now and again swoops out to snap up a fly, returning to the same perch.

At Helwith, ignore the footbridge and go a few steps beyond it, through the wooden gate, to ford the branching stream of Shaw Beck which dries up altogether in summer.

Helwith has seven or eight footpaths leading to it and a manor house, indicating its former importance in leadmining days. It once had a grammar school founded by John Bathurst in 1659 which successfully gave free education to all children in the village for more than 200 years. It offered the three Rs, geography, history and 'other useful branches of learning'.

The path follows Shaw Beck now, over the short clipped grass of a rabbit warren, where there are many holes of a large colony, and where spring sandwort and mountain pansy grow together. The mountain pansies here have creamy-white upper petals and the lower ones yellow, yet another variety of this lovely wild flower. In late March, a bank on the right is smoth-ered in hundreds of primroses, though by summer they are replaced by bracken fronds.

Signs of leadmining come into view. Tips of fine-grained material are the result of crushing and enriching the ore by sorting out the gangue – the white sparry minerals thrown on the tip heaps as waste. An eleven-bay bouse store was for the rough ore as it came from the mine. You can find bits of galena, chert, calcite and barite on the tips, and dissolved fossils occur as moulds in the sandy limestone, while wheatear, meadow pipit, grey and pied wagtails accompany you upstream.

Cross the small packhorse bridge, pass the entrance to the level of the Prys lead-mine and take the left fork up a narrow gill. Some 12-14,000 years ago, floodwaters from melting glaciers surged down this way, continued down Shaw Beck and into Marske Beck. A great volume of meltwater was responsible for carving out the deep and steep-sided, winding form of these valleys.

Make your way up and out of the gill, via two wooden gates, across a farm track and left by a metal gate. The way is up the hill

Wild thyme indicates limestone near the surface.

A waterwheel at Pillimire Bridge, Marske.

(south-west) with a wall on the left to start with, past a barn and left of a fence to the top of the field. Low Greenas Farm is on the right. Left along the wall is a red wooden gate. Take the path through the gate, past the corrugated iron barn of High Greenas Farm, to two gates at the end of a tarred road (Helwith Road) coming in from the right.

Here at 1,150 feet (350m) above sea level is the meeting place of five old roads. Take the route straight on across the heather of Skelton Moor, following a wall on the right. This was an old lead road bringing lead ore to the Clints smelt mills from the ancient Hurst mining area. It is lapwing and curlew country and, if you haven't already see either, then you are likely to come across them here. One of the plovers, the lapwing is a strikingly hand-some bird in the breeding season, with its long crest and contrasting black, white and bronzy-green plumage. On the ground, you may see one tilt forward to peck at a morsel and reveal an orange patch under the tail. The curlew is another wader, but twice as big as the lapwing. Its conspicuous long, down-curved bill, streaky brown plumage

and whitish, triangular rump distinguish it. Both birds are best known for the sounds they make, and their names of peewit and curlew imitate their calls.

The distant view ahead is of the jaws of Swaledale at Richmond, the aerial masts and Willance's Leap, and the junction of Marske Beck and the Swale. The moor comes abruptly to an end, and the path follows the edge of the Marske Valley with a wonderful view of this peaceful dale. Keep straight on to a metal gate and walled lane to the road at Skelton, a hamlet of a few cottages. Turn right along the road for 150 yards (135m), then left over a stile and diagonally across a field. There are two further stiles and some fine mature oak trees as you approach Pillimire Bridge. Just by the beck above the bridge is an inter-esting waterwheel still in position. The packhorse bridge is not on a main road or trade route, and has survived in its original state.

Cross Pillimire Bridge and follow the beck downstream on the left bank, finally passing through a patch of mature wood-land, containing large oaks and beeches, to step up onto the ancient Marske Bridge.

WALK 5: MARRICK AND THE PRIORY FROM DOWNHOLME BRIDGE

Start: Downholme Bridge. Grid Ref: 113 992
Distance: 7½ miles (12km)
OS Maps: Outdoor Leisure 30 or Landranger 99
Walking Time: 3½ to 4 hours

Good footpaths make the going easy, through farmland and woods, to finish along the riverside. The walk visits the small village of Marrick, descends the Nuns' Causey in Steps Wood (a notable bird locality) to Marrick Priory, and returns on an interesting route above the Swale. The best parking place is by the A6108 about 300 yards (275m) on the Richmond side of Downholme Bridge.

The car park mentioned above is backed by a steep bank of limestone scree where common spotted orchid, wild strawberries and many other interesting plants grow. Downholme Scar has several mentions in Baker's book on flora, *North Yorkshire*, and one or two rare sedges grow nearby. In 1816, the great artist Turner journeyed this way before the turnpike road was built in 1836. He came over the moors from Bolton Castle in Wensleydale to Grinton, made a drawing of Marrick Priory and forded the river to Ellerton. He passed through Downholme and Hudswell to Richmond.

Downholme Bridge has three arches, each one bigger than the last, as it carries the road from Marske uphill to the main A6108. Until the 1680s there wasn't a road across the Swale between Richmond and Grinton. The road up the dale was through Marske on the north side of the valley. In 1684, John Hutton of Marske asked permission to build a bridge 'betwixt Dounham and Maske' and offered to pay much of the cost. That bridge was destroyed during the terrible floods of 1771, and rebuilt in 1773 by John Carr, surveyor of bridges for the North Riding. There are a number of interesting masons' marks on the stones under the arches.

From the bridge, take the road towards Marske and, about 100 yards (90m) beyond the bend and the first bridleway (the return route), enter a cultivated field on the left along a second bridleway. Follow the path up the hill, gradually approaching the wood and limestone scar on the right. Pass in front of the abandoned farmhouse of Low Hollings, surrounded by musk thistles, and follow a well-built, seven foot (2.1m) limestone wall, on the right, all the way to Hollins Farm, over half a mile (1km) further on. Up on the right is an old deer park, former gallops for racehorses, and crowning the highest point is the Hutton Monument. At Gallop End is a double limekiln with two arches, and along the track grows goat's beard, a large yellow daisy-flower which produces a fine downy 'clock' like that of the dandelion. Its other name is Jack-go-to-bed-at-noon, which refers to its habit of flowering in the morning and closing up around midday.

The path leads you round the farmhouse and through the yard, passing out to the left where it joins the Coast-to-Coast long distance footpath, founded by Wainwright. Between here and the priory you are sure to meet walkers staggering along under heavy packs, having completed at least half of their 190 mile (300 km) journey between St Bees Head and Robin Hood's Bay.

From Hollins Farm go forward, take the gate on the left and go diagonally across the fields, over Ellers Beck, full of beautiful water crowfoot. Half a mile (800m) higher up this beck (though not on our route) is Marske smelt mill, one of the best preserved in Swaledale. Pass in front of the lonely cottage of Ellers. The old meadows ahead contain yellow rattle and the yellow-flowering meadow vetchling. The latter is a valuable plant to have in a meadow as, not only does it fix nitrogen into the soil, but, as cattle food, is also rich in protein.

The Coast-to-Coast path is clearly waymarked and easy to follow, though the approach to Marrick village is rather circuitous. But once onto the 'main street', turn left at the telephone box, bear round to the right and through the lower part of the village. Marrick has many old farms, barns and leadminers' cottages, stands 1,000 feet (300m) above sea level and faces south. In contrast to many Swaledale villages, it is well spread out. In earlier days it was an important centre, having many routes leading to it and being on the only road up the dale to Reeth and Muker.

Pass two former chapels; then the sunken path descends to the margin of Steps Wood, where there is a first view of Marrick Priory. Since the village had no church, the people took this path to the priory church, right up to the present century, so it has become a well-trodden parishioners' way. It is known as the 'Nuns' Causey' as the 375 steps through the wood are as old as the priory.

The wood is a notable site for birds, and has a breeding population of great spotted and green woodpeckers, garden warbler and wood warbler, willow warbler and chiffchaff, and also nuthatch. Both spotted and pied flycatchers may be seen as well as the more common residents. The most distinctive feature of the garden warbler is its beautiful song, rather like that of the blackcap's but more mellow, faster and even longer. This shy and sombre-

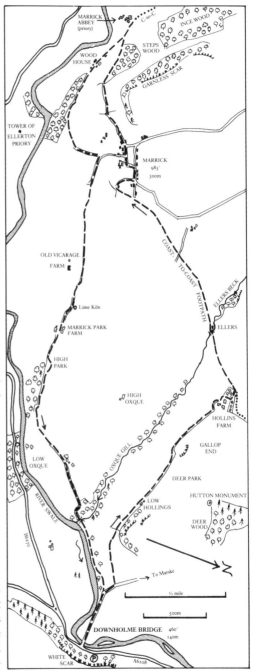

53

The age-old path through Steps Wood to Marrick Priory.

coloured bird prefers thickets of brambles and undergrowth to a garden. In the autumn it builds up its strength on black-berries – in Yorkshire it is said to have a special liking for cherries – before returning to the forest savannas of Africa.

Standing prominently above the Swale, Marrick Priory (or Abbey) was built in 1154 as a Benedictine nunnery. Dissolution came in 1540, but the old nave continued to be used for church services. A farmstead was built on the south side, making use of stone from the ruins, then in 1811 the church was rebuilt from the nave. Only the tower now remains of the original structure. In the 1960s the whole place became an outdoor education centre of the Ripon

Diocese, and visitors are welcome to look round the grounds.

There are few records of the priory, though in 1252 the prioress was told to treat her nuns kindly and to correct their faults privately. Leave from the abbey was granted in special circumstances, but only if accompanied by a prudent and mature nun. In the 1530s a beautiful young woman, dressed as a man, arrived exhausted on the doorstep. Isabella Beaufort had secretly fled from the Court and the attentions of Henry VIII, disguised as a page boy. She was taken in by the nuns, and remained for a few years until her real lover discovered her whereabouts. They were married at the time of the Dissolution in

An engraving (published in 1823) of Marrick Priory from a dramatised watercolour by Turner after his visit in 1816.

1540, when Marrick had a prioress and sixteen nuns.

From the priory, turn down the dale along the track past Wood Farm and up to a narrow walled lane. From the entrance to the lane there is a good view of the fifteenth century tower, all that remains of Ellerton Priory just across the river. This was an even smaller nunnery of Cistercian foundation, and many of its records and charters were lost in fourteenth century raids by the Scots. At the time of the Dissolution there were only five nuns living there.

Turn right at the top of the lane and along the track, quite close to Marrick village again, and keep up through three fields and on to another farm track coming in from the left. There are good views of the valley and, just before Park Farm, a double limekiln on the left with a bank of primroses and celandine in the spring.

Beyond the farm is a bouldery area of the Main limestone dotted with bushes of elderflower. Pass alongside hay meadows where yellow rattle, meadow vetchling and the slender yellow spikes of agrimony grow, while on the right a bushy area reaches down to the river. Goldfinches and swallows are to be seen at Low Oxque, and the route joins a leafy lane which descends to a riverside track, a delightful stretch of the river and a popular site for picnics. The path comes out onto the road and Downholme Bridge is straight ahead.

WALK 6: MAIDEN CASTLE, HARKERSIDE AND GRINTON

Start: Reeth. Grid Ref: 038 993
Distance: 8 miles (13km)
OS Maps: Outdoor Leisure 30 or Landranger 98
Walking Time: 4 hours

This is a great walk, not to be missed. From Reeth, it includes a secluded stretch of the river, visits the prehistoric remains of Maiden Castle and climbs the slopes of Harkerside to open moor. Further impressive earthworks are to be seen on the way down to the lovely village of Grinton. See the 'cathedral of the Dales' and return by the Swale at its widest. The going can be rough in places and the climb from the river, though not too steep, amounts to 930 feet (284m). The walk is especially good for birds and prehistory. There is parking around the green in Reeth.

Reeth is an important centre for Swaledale, being situated in a superb position at the junction with Arkengarthdale. With its charter granted in 1695, Reeth's cobbled square and spacious green were the focus of an important market in the eighteenth and nineteenth centuries, when leadmining flourished and hand-knitting prospered. Several hotels, eating places and fine old houses line up round the green, the Swaledale Folk Museum exhibits items of local history and there is the Reeth agricultural show in late August.

Go past Barclays Bank at the top corner of the green to a narrow snicket where there is a sign 'to the river'. Turn left through the modern bungalows, and then right along Quaker Lane and past the doctor's surgery. A Quaker school was built along here about 1788 with money from three Raw brothers. Children from the whole town could attend. It was replaced in 1862, with a legacy from another John Raw, by the bigger Friends' school which can be seen on the hill above the village, where pupils in the top class could even learn geology and mining.

At the lane end, turn left towards the river and bear right to the recently repaired suspension bridge, known as the 'swing bridge'. The river floods regularly here, and evidence of erosion can be seen below the footbridge while, further over, banks of gravel have been deposited, changing the course of the main channel. Oystercatchers find nesting sites among the pebbles, and sand martins make holes in the sandy riverbank. Keep an eye open along the river for goosander which, in June, may be accompanied by its young. The female has a reddish-brown head and grey body, the head of the male is dark green and the body black and white. Both have a flattish crest and a long, slender red bill. The yellow wagtail, too, inhabits this part of the river. Its brilliant yellow underparts and long tail make it conspicuous, and its greenish-brown back distinguishes it from the grey wagtail.

Cross the bridge and look back up the slopes to the school. The farming terraces, or strip lynchets, are clearly seen and are thought to have been developed particularly in the thirteenth century when the climate was warmer and cultivation of crops was extended up the slopes. It is possible that the original pattern of terraces was initiated by Anglian farmers in the eighth century. The constant ploughing of strips in one direction pulled earth into the

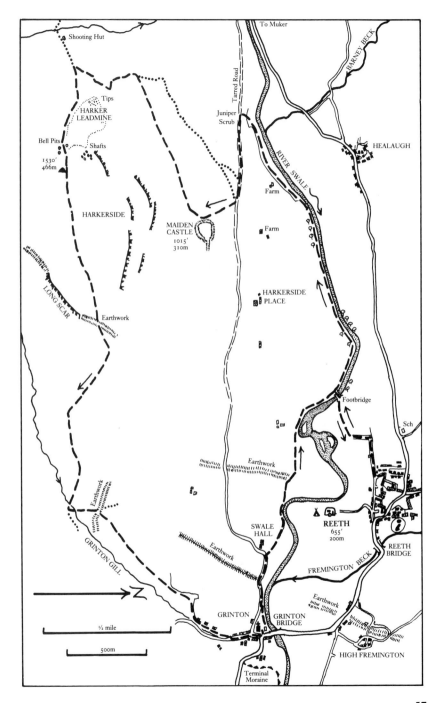

Shooting Hut

Tips

HARKER
LEADMINE

Bell Pits

Shafts

1530'
466m

HARKERSIDE

LONG SCAR

Earthwork

Earthwork

Earthwork

GRINTON GILL

½ mile

500m

MAIDEN
CASTLE
1015'
310m

To Muker

Tarred Road

Juniper
Scrub

RIVER SWALE

BARNEY BECK

HEALAUGH

Farm

Farm

HARKERSIDE
PLACE

Footbridge

Sch

Earthwork

SWALE
HALL

REETH
655'
200m

REETH
BRIDGE

FREMINGTON BECK

Earthwork

GRINTON

GRINTON
BRIDGE

HIGH FREMINGTON

Terminal
Moraine

terrace pattern, and stones turned up by the plough were put to reinforce the steep slope between one terrace and the next.

Walk upstream along the tree-lined bank, raised against flooding. You may be lucky and see a mink foraging through the grass. They can appear fearless and are seen as much out of the water as in it. The thick, glossy coat, almost black in colour, is a reminder that the ancestors of these animals were farmed for their fur.

Climb up away from the river at the fingerpost, pass through a wooden gate in a fine drystone wall with huge 'footings' in its base, and up to the road. Here is a quiz question: what plant is common in Swaledale but does not grow in Wensleydale? The answer is juniper, which here spreads right across the hillside. The bush, one of Britain's native conifers, grows with heather, bilberry and bracken, not unlike patches of juniper scrub in Scotland. The leaves contain an aromatic oil and the berries are used to flavour gin and jugged hare. In days gone by, chips of juniper wood were burned to fumigate houses against the plague.

This is sparrowhawk country, where the agile predators are on the look-out for small birds like meadow pipits, willow warblers, red polls and linnets that find cover in the juniper.

Turn up the road, from where there are extensive views up and down the dale. After 330 yards (300m), just past Stubbins Farm and a wall corner on the left, there is a sign for Castle Bolton. Ignore this and go to the left of it, heading straight up the moor to a hawthorn tree on the horizon. The tree is growing in the ditch of Maiden Castle, a formidable prehistoric earthwork, variously described as a Bronze Age henge or an Iron Age hill fort. It is squarish in shape with curved sides, measuring 120 by 100 yards (110×90m), with a deep ditch and embankment all the way round. Walk round the ditch to the other side, where the entrance has two parallel banks of stones leading to it. The whole thing is large and impressive, and must have required a lot of organisation and effort in its construction, probably by Iron Age people before the arrival of the Romans. A large green burial mound is situated at the far end of the stone avenue and there is a tradition that gold is buried beneath it. Perhaps the uneven surface is from diggings for the precious metal.

Looking across Maiden Castle from the tumulus, you can make out a cairn on a hillock to the west. This is the next goal. From here the path is non-existent, so follow the contour in the same direction (west-south-west) to the foot of a bare leadmine tip heap which juts out. Mossy saxifrage grows stuntedly in the gravel of the tip. Beyond this, join a double track which aims for a wooden shooting box; but before reaching it, turn left, almost doubling back on a less well-worn bridleway that leads up above the mine workings and hushes to the top of Harkerside.

Several neat, grass-covered bell pits decorate the top of the hill and can afford some shelter in strong winds. To the right the heather moors extend to the horizon, territory of the golden plover and meadow pipit. In the other direction across the dale are Calver Hill, Fremington Edge and Arkengarthdale, and in the distance Darlington and the Cleveland Hills – a wonderful panorama.

The gentle downhill gradient along the top of Harkerside helps in making good headway to its brow, where there is a large stone embankment with a ditch below it. In his *The History of Swaledale* Edmund Cooper suggests that this earthwork was built by the Brigantes and intended as a hill-fort, possibly after their defeat by the Romans at Stanwick. There is a 350 yard (320m) length of it here, with steep natural

Calver Hill and Healaugh village from Harkerside.

scars at each end. There is an apparent continuation of the fortification towards Reeth, near to the river and a further length on the Fremington side. Whether, or for how long, this great rampart halted the Roman legions we shall never know.

Descend to the right and fork right down to Grinton Gill. Just before the beck there is the site of a small dam and evidence of iron smelting, with pieces of slag, reddened rocks and a large chunk of cast iron.

Go through the gate in the fence, and turn down the stream and immediately over it, to a track which leads to another huge earth embankment, a further section of the Brigantian defences. Go straight on at this point, bearing a little to the right to follow the left side of Grinton Gill down a good

path to Grinton village. The path passes some old cottages along the beckside before crossing a stone bridge. The small and attractive village of Grinton has some of the best traditional cottages in Swaledale, with doorway dates going back to 1648 and 1666. Blackburn Hall, next to the church, is a remarkable old building with stone-mullioned windows and tall chimneys, being formerly the home of the Blackburn family and lords of Grinton, who had a chapel in the church.

Grinton Church was founded in Norman times by the monks of Bridlington, and is dedicated to St Andrew. Known as the 'Cathedral of the Dales' it was built to serve a large parish stretching to the head of the dale. Parishioners had far to come to

Grinton Church was formerly the parish church for the whole of the upper dale.

church, so market day was on a Sunday to save an added journey during the week. When a funeral was required for somebody from Keld, it took two days to bring the body along the Corpse Road.

The church is a very fine Perpendicular building, with much Norman and thirteenth and fourteenth century work. It is full of treasures and interesting features: for example, its Norman window and font, grooves in the porch made by the sharpening of swords and arrows, a leper's squint to allow people outside to view the alter, a chained Bible on a fourteenth century wooden stand and ancient window glass.

Of the people of Grinton, we hear that in 1609 they were charged for not repairing the highway between Witaside and Richmond. In 1604, John Maye was fined for keeping an unlicensed alehouse and, in 1613, John Blades and others were fined for riotous assembly and assault on the wife and servant of George Alderson. Another Grinton man was made to stand on the pillory at Richmond for stealing deer. In

the early days of cricket, Grinton had a team which, in September 1848, had a resounding victory over a combined eleven in Wensleydale. They won by an innings and twenty-four 'notches', runs being scored by cutting notches on a stick.

Pass round the sixteenth century church tower, to leave the churchyard by a small wooden gate for the short footpath up the river to the road. Arkle Beck joins the River Swale just above this point, and the view from the road is of a deeper and more mature river. It is a good place for birds, and in the summer you can compare sand martins with house martins, and swallows with swifts, as they all dart about over the water.

After 330 yards (300m) along the road, turn right onto a narrow walled lane. Swale Hall, just above this point, was for 300 years the home of the noble Swale family. The Swales were descended from Walter de Gant, kinsman to William the Conquerer and holder of the manor of Healaugh. Several members of the family had distinguished careers through the centuries. In 1660, the loyalist Solomon Swale MP was the man who, in the House of Commons, proposed the restoration of Charles II as king. About a hundred years later the Swales had omitted to renew their lease on Swale Hall, and in the 1770s another Sir Solomon Swale had the estate and leadmines fraudulently taken from him by a clerk who had discovered the lapse. Sir Solomon spent all his money on lawsuits and died in a debtor's prison in 1773. Swale Hall was then sold as a farmhouse.

From the lane, continue near the river. The lane is the haunt of the redstart and, as you approach the riverside, oystercatchers may be heard again and ever more sand martins.

Cross the 'swing bridge' and retrace your steps to the right, up the narrow lane and back to Reeth.

WALK 7: LOWER ARKENGARTHDALE, HURST AND FREMINGTON EDGE

Start: Reeth. Grid Ref: 038 993
Distance: 7½ miles (12km)
OS Maps: Outdoor Leisure 30 or Landranger 92 and 98
Walking Time: 4 hours

This is an exhilarating walk exploring lower Arkengarthdale, climbing up onto Fremington Edge, visiting the former mining village of Hurst and descending to High Fremington. It includes a lovely valley walk, a woodland bird habitat, a steepish climb, some leadmining history, heather moors and, in clear weather, very fine views. There is parking round the green in Reeth.

The picturesque village of Reeth lies in a commanding position on sunny slopes at the foot of Calver Hill, where Arkengarthdale meets Swaledale, and about halfway from Richmond to Keld. It is of Anglian origins, though there is much evidence of Romano-British settlement nearby. It has long been the main focus of the dale, a centre for markets, fairs and, of course, for leadmining. It was a thriving little town in the eighteenth and early nineteenth centuries, and the fine Georgian buildings reflect wealth from the lead trade. In 1851 the population was 1,350, but a hundred years later had dropped to 580.

Today Reeth is a busy tourist centre and makes an excellent starting point for walks along both valleys, over the moors of Harkerside and Grinton to the south, for exploring Reeth and Marrick moors on the north side, or the magnificent limestone scarp of Fremington Edge.

Starting in Reeth, make for the corner of the green to the right of the Burgoyne Hotel and past the Wesleyan chapel. Nearby is Harland House, where, in Victorian times, Captain John Harland lived. He is best remembered for his glossary of the Swaledale dialect and the verses about Reeth Bartle Fair. The latter recalls the fair of St Bartholomew's Day, when the lead-

miners spent their hard-earned cash and forgot their humdrum lives.

Turn to the right between the houses, where a steep road leads down to Arkle Beck. Walk down the beckside to Reeth Bridge, going under the bridge, then over it. This fine stonework was constructed across Arkle Beck in 1773 by John Carr, Bridge Master of the North Riding and architect of Harewood House, north of Leeds. The new bridge replaced one destroyed by the great floods two years previously.

On the left, what is now a garage and petrol station was the old stables and sawmill for the leadmines, once owned by the Denys family. Go through a stile ahead and immediately left through the fields with Fremington Edge up on the right, the White House conspicuous on its slopes. This is the beginning of Arkengarthdale, originally part of a hunting forest of the Norman lords. It was never a rich farming area, but became particularly important for leadmining. In 1656 Dr John Bathurst, physician to Oliver Cromwell, purchased mines in Arkengarthdale and his son Charles became a famous mine owner. The CB leadmines and Charles Bathurst Hotel are named after him.

Veer away from Arkle Beck, and up

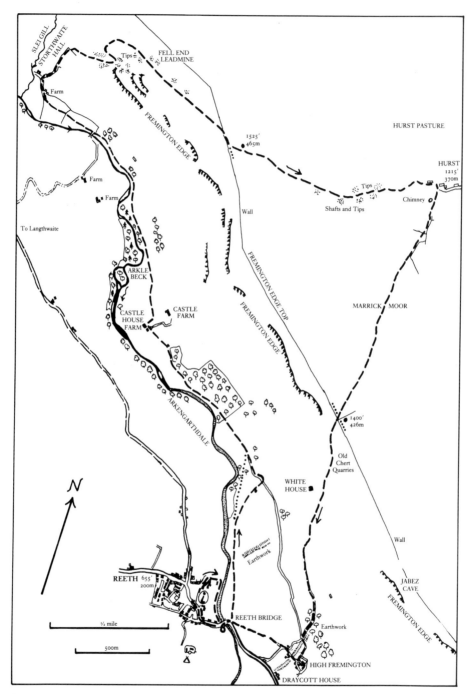

SLEI GILL

STORTHWAITE HALL

FELL END LEADMINE

Tips

Farm

FREMINGTON EDGE

HURST PASTURE

1525'
465m

HURST
1215'
370m

Wall

Tips

Chimney

Shafts and Tips

Farm

Farm

To Langthwaite

ARKLE BECK

FREMINGTON EDGE TOP

FREMINGTON EDGE

MARRICK MOOR

CASTLE HOUSE FARM

CASTLE FARM

ARKENGARTHDALE

1400'
426m

Old Chert Quarries

N

WHITE HOUSE

Wall

Earthwork

JABEZ CAVE

REETH 655'
200m

FREMINGTON EDGE

½ mile

REETH BRIDGE

Earthwork

500m

HIGH FREMINGTON

DRAYCOTT HOUSE

62

The blackcap is known as the 'northern nightingale' because of its lovely song.

through two squeezer stiles past a barn. The path here is an overgrown paved way from a mine higher up. Turn left along a bridleway, where scattered hawthorns dot the hummocky slopes of Fremington Edge. Pass a limekiln on the right just before the wood, where the built-up path winds between some fine ash trees and dead elms.

These little patches of woodland are a haven for many birds. Summer visitors which nest here include the willow warbler, wood warbler, blackcap, redstart and spotted flycatcher. If you are trying to memorise some bird songs, the willow warbler's is a good one to start with. A very common bird in the late spring and early summer, it is difficult to see, but its pure, descending notes and chirrup are so frequently heard that it is easy to learn. The blackcap's short song is rich and varied, clearly phrased and a beautiful sound on a

still day. The wood warbler makes a quiet but accelerating *stip-stip-stip* ending in a shivering trill *shreeee*.

Stay near the lower side of the wood, then pass the decaying ruin of a charming old farmhouse, nicely built with an outside two-seater toilet, and beautifully situated facing the sun in a tranquil woodland setting. Castle House Farm follows, where a green lane leads up to Castle Farm, a typical 'longhouse' on the hillside. The view in the other direction is to Calver Hill and the road up Arkengarthdale.

Cross the lane and go to the right of Castle House Farm, through the fields, following the yellow spots, with a low-lying area on the left known as Thorndale. This is a sheltered spot where you may see oystercatcher, grey wagtail or heron. Dark green alders are followed by tall pines and larches, and new tree saplings grow in a

A green lane leads to Castle Farm, Arkengarthdale.

small enclosure. Near the river, a wet patch reveals wet-loving plants such as kingcups, monkey flower, water mint and horsetail. The great spotted woodpecker taps away on the branches of the dead trees and, in the autumn, siskins feed on the alders near the beck.

Come out of the trees and, after the wooden footbridge, fork right, away from the river, through a gate gap to the farm. Growing on the riverbank are the purple blooms of the opium poppy, a garden escape but once much valued on farms for its non-narcotic seeds, still used for cooking. Pass in front of the farm and on to the cottage known as Stourthwaite Hall, where the delightful gardens, window boxes and hanging baskets are bursting with colour.

Turn right here up the bridleway signed 'to Hurst', up to the top of the field and through the wooden gate. On the far side of the wall, turn right alongside a hush and an area of leadmining activity of Fell End Mine. The hush is a man-made gully,

scoured by sending repeated torrents of water down it to reveal the lead ore.

Wheatears inhabit these parts, where they like the rocky outcrops, drystone walls or a hole among some large stones to build their loose grassy nests. The Dales landscape provides well for them and so they are fairly common and easily seen, the white rump being very noticeable.

The mine tailings – the waste products of mining – contain good specimens of barite and galena. The heavy, white mineral barite consists of barium sulphate. In powdered form it is used in a barium meal – because it is particularly dense it shows up internal organs on X-ray photographs. The ore the miners were after was galena, or lead sulphide. It is a dull grey until freshly broken, when it has a silvery shine to it. Being three times as dense as limestone, galena can be found by picking up a rock with some grey patches on it and 'weighing' it in the hand.

The path swings to the left up the hill and onto the top of the escarpment. From here there are wonderful views across to Booze, where there are improved pastures, then North Rake hush in Slei Gill, and grouse moors which show up as a patchwork due to the methodical burning of the heather by the gamekeepers.

Walk up to the right, in an easterly direction, through the mine tips, gradually moving away from Fremington Edge. Cairns top one or two of the spoil heaps, marking the route, and you can find lovely pink pieces of barite scattered about. Cross the broken-down wall and walk due east along a green 'ribbon' through the heather. In the distance are two chimney stacks which mark the small community of Hurst. Further spoil heaps carry ironstone nodules and fossil corals.

Two gates bring you into Hurst, which grew in the seventeenth century as a new village, a direct result of expansion in the leadmining industry. Beneath the surface was a complex of rich lead veins and Hurst became the only settlement in the area situated close to the mines. From a thriving community of more than forty houses including the Green Dragon Inn, it has become a 'lost village' with just a farm and two or three cottages left among ruins amid a bleak scene of spoil heaps. The altitude of 1,200 feet (370m) above sea level and the distance from main roads accelerated the decline. But there is no doubt that mining at Hurst goes back at least to Roman times and that it was once the hub of the industry.

Turn right through two iron gates where mountain pansies line the double track and pass to the left of the square chimney stack. Beyond the second gate the route leads through the open heather moor, climbing slowly towards the Edge once again. This unassuming track is an unclassified county highway, and as such is not marked as a right of way on OS maps. To the left are extensive views eastwards to Richmond, the gateway of Swaledale, and the Vale of Mowbray and Cleveland Hills beyond.

On approaching the Edge, go forward through the wooden gate in the wall and down the winding road to High Fremington. Magnificent views of Reeth, Swaledale and Arkengarthdale present themselves, before a descent past the White House and a wayside spring. The track is tarred from here on. High up on the Edge is Jabez Cave. A shopkeeper of Reeth, Jabez Raisbeck was a poet and in the 1890s would retreat to this peaceful place near the top of Fremington Edge to write his verses.

Approaching High Fremington and immediately beyond a narrow walled path to the right, look for the Iron Age earth embankment that crosses the line of the little road. There is a sideways view of it a little further on and, on turning right after the first cottages of High Fremington, the earthwork again crosses your path. It carries on down the slope and through the fields on the other side of the main road, almost to the river, where the Arkle joins the Swale. The embankment on the other side of the Swale, seen on walk 6, is in a direct line with this one.

The village of Fremington is now a quiet little hamlet but it once had a school that served the whole of the parish of Grinton. It was founded in 1643 and thrived for over 400 years with, in 1811, as many as 130 scholars. In the seventeenth century, Sir Thomas Elliot of Fremington was one of the main advocates of the enclosure of land for scientific management. From the main road can be seen the Georgian frontage of Draycott House, former home of the Denys family, wealthy leadmine owners.

Where the narrow road from High Fremington curves down to the left, fork right via a gated stile and field path down to Reeth Bridge. Cross the bridge and continue along the road and up into Reeth village.

WALK 8: WINDEGG SCAR, BOOZE AND SLEI GILL FROM LANGTHWAITE

Start: Langthwaite. Grid Ref: 005 025
Distance: 5½ miles (9km)
OS Maps: Outdoor Leisure 30 or Landranger 92
Walking Time: 3 hours

This remarkably varied and interesting walk takes you through wooded scars, climbs up beneath the limestone cliffs of Windegg Scar, visits Booze and the small leadmining valley of Slei Gill, to return alongside Arkle Beck to the pretty village of Langthwaite. The village is not on a bus route and parking is limited to a few places on the main road.

For centuries Arkengarthdale was a hunting forest which passed from the Saxon kings to the Normans and the care of Robert Arkhil, when the area became known as Arkhil Garth. The name still appears in Arkle Town and Arkle Beck. From the 1700s the dale took on an important role in the leadmining industry and Langthwaite was established as its main centre. Here, old leadminers' cottages huddle round the small square and the Red Lion pub looks placidly on. The picturesque bridge over the Arkle is familiar to many who saw it in the title sequence of the first television series of *All Creatures Great and Small*. Scenes from *A Woman of Substance* were also filmed nearby.

Higher up on the main road stand the cottages of High Green, the parish church and the fine building of the Methodist chapel (1882). The church was built in 1818, to replace the one in Arkle Town that became neglected. It is the only example in the Dales of a 'commissioners' church', built by funds from Parliament (with additional help from local benefactors) raised after the defeat of Napoleon at Waterloo. The new buildings were known as Waterloo churches and were very simple in design, with no pictorial windows.

From the centre of Langthwaite, go up through the village and left on a bridleway along the lower edge of a wood. This is a characteristic Dales ash wood on limestone, clothing Langthwaite Scar with wych elm, sycamore and occasional yew trees. The woods between here and Scar House are notable for breeding wood warblers, pied flycatchers and redstarts, as well as woodpeckers and nuthatches. You may be thrilled by the piercing notes of the familiar song thrush echoing through the trees, but to see the little handsome pied flycatcher in its acrobatic flight as it dives for flies is a joy to any observer.

The flowers of Scar House Woods are a colourful mixture of primroses, violets, greater stitchwort, bluebells and red campion, with occasional early purple orchids. Dog's mercury and wild garlic (or ramsons) can cover large patches of the woodland floor, the latter exuding an oniony perfume in the spring.

The path continues along the narrow, walled Windegg Lane above the wood, where mature beeches and pines grow, gradually climbing past an abandoned cottage and eventually out onto open moor. Keep straight on, past a sheepfold where the path peters out, and if you find yourself gravitating towards the road on the left,

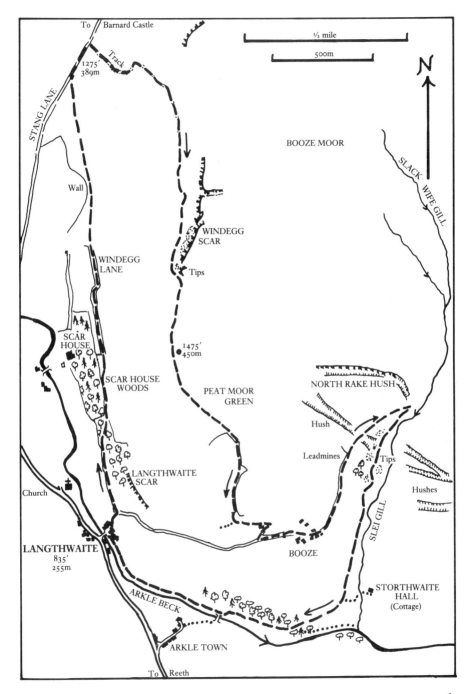

To Barnard Castle

½ mile

500m

N

1275'
389m

Track

STANG LANE

BOOZE MOOR

SLACK WIFE GILL

Wall

WINDEGG SCAR

WINDEGG LANE

Tips

SCAR HOUSE

1475'
450m

SCAR HOUSE WOODS

PEAT MOOR GREEN

NORTH RAKE HUSH

Hush

Leadmines

Tips

Hushes

LANGTHWAITE SCAR

Church

SLEI GILL

LANGTHWAITE
835'
255m

BOOZE

STORTHWAITE HALL
(Cottage)

ARKLE BECK

ARKLE TOWN

To Reeth

67

Windegg Scar.

walk up the road to the bridleway sign which points up a double stony track towards the scar.

The white limestone of Windegg Scar is interrupted by buff-coloured buttresses where the rock has become dolomitised. The original limestone has chemically absorbed magnesium from the ancient seawater to form dolomite, a variety of limestone named after the Dolomites in northern Italy. Not only has the rock changed colour but it has shrunk to produce hollows which are filled with hexagonal calcite crystals, some with flattened ends (nailhead) and others with long sharp points (dogtooth).

There is a great length of opencast lead-mines along the base of the scar which were opened up by Dr John Bathurst. In 1682, it was claimed the mines were yielding a profit of twice the rent. Physician to Oliver Cromwell, John Bathurst bought land in the area and he, his son Charles and descendants became an important leadmining family. The fine scar scenery to the left is complemented on the right by magnificent views up and down Arkengarthdale.

Follow the track, keeping straight on where it doubles back to the left, then continue across the open Peat Moor Green to an intake wall. Keep the wall on the right and descend an old sunken track, branching left along a short walled lane to a ruined farm. Flowers here in the early summer include spring sandwort, a mass of mountain pansies and shining cranesbill.

Zigzag down into Booze. This hamlet was described by the Victorian writer Harry Speight as 'clinging to the hill like a tipsy man to a lamp-post'. But, although there were once forty miners' cottages here, there was never an ale house or inn and, what's more, the Methodist inhabitants were enthusiastic abstainers. Methodism was strong in Booze in the early 1800s and meetings were held regularly. However, the chapel which was planned for the village was eventually built in Langthwaite in 1839. Like Hurst, it was essentially a mining community which declined dramatically in the 1880s, and today consists of just a few farms. The name of Booze is now thought to be derived from 'bull house'.

Continue curving to the left into Slei Gill alongside a walled lane, now completely grown over with vegetation. Cross Tanner Rake Hush, pass the entrance to a mining level, a horizontal tunnel into the hillside, and go below a small barn. Descend to a wall built down the centre of North Rake Hush and double back here on a lower, green miners' track down this peaceful little valley.

Three big lead veins in the Main limestone pass through this part of the gill, and as a result there is a concentrated knot of hushes, shafts and levels. The veins may have been known at a very early date. The tip heaps contain the minerals barite and galena, and fossil crinoids (ringed, worm-like shapes). There are also moulds of lampshells in the silty limestones and chert, and on the fine-grained slabs of rock

Calver Hill from Windegg Scar.

(which split easily) you can pick out the curved pattern left by a burrowing and feeding sea creature known as *Zoophicos*, a trace fossil which is quite common in the Swaledale area. The soft-bodied animal grazed in ever-increasing circles, leaving the swirling marks like a cock's tail.

Pink wild roses are scattered along the slopes of the gill and the bright starry white flowers of spring sandwort dot the ground. In May or June you could catch sight of a cuckoo which may have laid an egg in each of a dozen nests of the unsuspecting little meadow pipit. It is the male cuckoo that makes the far-carrying call. Small tortoise-shell, peacock butterflies and small coppers are on the wing. In September you are even more likely to see these three, which include second broods from eggs laid in the summer.

A view of the stepped outline of Calver Hill lies ahead as the well-built track wends its way down through the spoil heaps. Cross a wooden stile in a fence, and Slei Gill opens out to meet the tree-lined Arkle. Ignore the left turn to Fremington and bear right through a gate into mature mixed woodland, where tall beeches and pines form a high canopy. On approaching Arkle Beck, pass a wooden footbridge (the path to Arkle Town) and continue along the beck-side to Langthwaite.

WALK 9: UPPER ARKENGARTHDALE

Start: Eskeleth: the road junction $^2/_3$ mile (1km) north of Langthwaite at the turn-off to Barnard Castle (the Stang Road). Grid Ref: 999 033
Distance: 7 miles (11km)
OS Maps: Outdoor Leisure Map 30 or Landranger 92
Walking Time: 3½ hours

After following Arkle Beck, a good place for wild flowers, and passing through the hamlet of Whaw, this delightful walk visits several remote hill farms on the edge of Arkengarthdale. It reaches open moor between Ravens Park and High Faggergill (good for birds) and returns to the beck to finish. The starting point is at the Barnard Castle road junction, 3¼ miles (6km) north of Reeth and $^2/_3$ mile (1km) north of Langthwaite. There is no public transport and parking is limited to the roadside near the junction.

Largely above 1,000 feet (305m), this land on the edge of heather moors was originally one of isolated Norse settlements, and has long been a sheep farming area. Many of the old farmhouses were built in the late seventeenth or eighteenth centuries. They faced south to take advantage of the sun, were very simple in design with two rooms and offshuts (or lean-to), and had farm buildings attached, all under a flagstone roof. There are still many working farms and the sheep are of the blackfaced variety, mainly Swaledales, which have fine horns on both tups and ewes, their long wool coats protecting them in the cold wet winters.

If you came up the road from Reeth or Langthwaite, you will have passed the Charles Bathurst Hotel. Long known as the CB Inn, it takes its name from the family who expanded leadmining in Arkengarthdale from about 1670. Completed in 1804, the Octagon Mill (the ruins can be seen above the road junction) was built to smelt ore from the Arkengarthdale mines. A thirty-six foot (11m) waterwheel worked the bellows for four furnaces. A fine piece of mining architecture, it was one of the best-known mine buildings in the Dales and was in good condition until the 1930s.

The well-preserved octagonal powder house on the lower side of the road was probably built about the same time as the mill.

Across the road from the CB Hotel is the school. Founded in 1659 by Dr John Bathurst, lord of the manor of Arkengarthdale, it was rebuilt in 1804 by George Brown and about that time had 150 scholars. It is still in use today.

Roadside verges are a sanctuary for many wild plants, and the margin of the road at the start of this walk is a noted locality for northern marsh orchid, which in June produces dense flower-spikes of rich purple with some lighter mottled shades. Some are so near the road that they are often flattened by passing vehicles. Ragged robin also grows here, and so care must be taken when parking.

Start by walking down the Stang Road (to Barnard Castle in Teesdale). It is unlikely that this road is of Roman origin, but it has been important since medieval times. It later became a main drove road along which thousands of cattle were herded from the Scottish borders; from Barnard Castle they came through Eskeleth and over to Low Row, and on to fairs at Askrigg, Leyburn or Middleham. On the

The white meadow saxifrage favours well-drained calcareous soils.

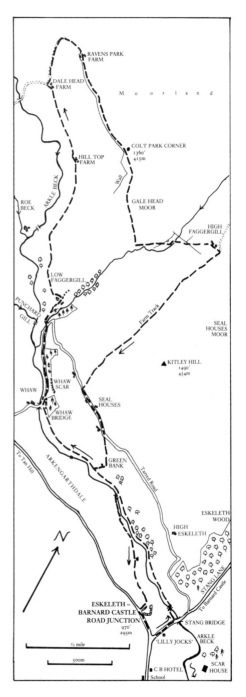

right is Plantation House, which 200 years ago was a drover's inn called Lilly Jocks.

Before Stang Bridge, take the squeezer stile to the left and, in June, look here for the lovely meadow saxifrage which has five white petals with green veins. After a hundred yards (90m) through the field, cross Arkle Beck by the footbridge and continue up the bank through fields where drystone walls contain large 'footings', huge rocks in the base of the wall. Pass into Eskeleth Wood, where ash, birch and alder grow, and bluebells, greater stitchwort and great woodrush cover the ground.

Whaw sits peacefully under the round-topped Kitlaw Hill.

A monolithic stone stile takes you back along the riverbank. Near the next foot-bridge is a bird cherry tree, which by July may be covered in the silken cobwebs made by caterpillars of the bird cherry ermine moth. Sometimes the tissue-like webs can envelop a whole tree, not an uncommon sight in Swaledale. Open ground with scattered trees is redstart country, and you may first know of their presence by the *weet* call, a single note sliding up the scale.

Arrive at the hamlet of Whaw, the last village in Arkengarthdale and 1,000 feet (300m) above sea level. The cluster of stone cottages, the newly-repaired little bridge, a few trees and the steep, rocky sides of the valley rising beyond form a picturesque Dales scene, one of apparent peace and seclusion. However, on 26th August 1986, the peace was shattered when extremely heavy rain on the moors – associated with Hurricane Charley – brought a devastatingly high wave of floodwater down Great Punchard Gill and into Arkle Beck, where it crashed into the stone bridge at Whaw, ripping away the top half of it.

Carry on upstream through Whaw, on a road with a steep bank, some of which is newly planted with trees. Where the road turns uphill to the right, keep straight on below the pine wood, along a farm track, to Low Faggergill, a good Norse name. The way round the farm is to fork right 100 yards (90m) before reaching it, along the track to High Faggergill, then to turn left through a field gate, skirting the rear of the farm, then right, through the middle of two fields with stiles. There is a view from here of Great Punchard Gill over to the left.

Cross two walls where the second stile is a yard or two higher up. The path reaches the top edge of the next field with a stile and gate. To the left, over the beck, is Shepherd's Lodge and ahead is a good view of Arkle Beck where the river has cut a square channel through glacial till.

Still on the same contour, continue across fields to pass through a gate in front of Hill Top Farm and, keeping well above the beck, another third of a mile (500m) to Dale Head Farm. Over this section of the walk there is an opportunity to see moorland birds such as the lapwing, redshank, snipe and curlew, as well as skylarks and wheatears. The redshank's orange-red legs and bill are easily seen when the bird is standing, but if alarmed it will take off, delivering a few loud piping notes and showing the white trailing edge to its curved wings. Another wader, the curlew, is twice as long at twenty-two inches (55cm), and its haunting call can be heard from February onwards as the melancholy *coour-lee* sound carries across open moor. The song consists of slow, then accelerating, liquid notes, ending in a bubbling trill.

Go to the left of Dale Head Farm and up the concrete strip-road which curves round through Ravens Park Farm. The path has turned direction, aims south-east and follows the moor edge above the intake wall. (This is the wall that separates the enclosed pastures from open moorland.) At the wall corner, known as Colt Park Corner, the route bears a little to the right

and fades out across Gale Head Moor. Press on (now south-south-east) until you reach a stream, turning left along a wall to cross a stile by a tumbled-down barn. Go over a gritstone slab bridge, then bear left up through the fields to High Faggergill farm, keeping to the right of it.

Higher up the valley of Faggergill is a former leadmine of the same name which was in production until about 1900. It then had a new lease of life between 1903 and 1910 when, for a time, it was producing ten tons of ore a month with a tramway bringing pony-drawn tubloads of ore to dressing floors near the mine entrance.

From Faggergill Farm, take the farm road down the valley. There are still snipe, lapwing and skylark to look out for, and wheatears which like to find nest holes among the scattered rocks. In fact the hillsides of upper Arkengarthdale appear to be well-strewn with rocks and boulders of all sizes.

The track becomes a tarred road and drops down to a road junction. Turn left for a quarter of a mile (400m) past two or three farms and cottages (of Seal Houses) to a gap in the wall on the right, signed 'footpath'. Descend diagonally down and to the left of Green Bank, a small cottage and to the riverbank. Turn left and cross the footbridge into a flowery meadow where yellow mountain pansies are dotted about a rabbit warren, and in the next field the tall, pink flowering stems of ragged robin grow among the rushes.

Leave the river after crossing a small stream and go through a renovated farmyard, up the track via Swallowholm cottages to the road and back to the starting point.

WALK 10: ROUND CALVER HILL FROM LANGTHWAITE

Start: Langthwaite. Grid Ref: 005 025
Distance: 7 miles (11km)
OS Maps: Outdoor Leisure 30 or Landranger 92 and 98
Walking Time: 3½ hours

Starting at the pretty village of Langthwaite, the walk follows an interesting section of Arkle Beck, including, on the return, a short tunnel. It visits Arkle Town, explores Fore Gill and traverses the moorland round Calver Hill, cutting in close to its steepest slopes. Some of the walking is over rough country where a map and compass may be useful. There is a fine place for flowers by the Arkle and moorland birds are especially good on the upland part of the walk. Parking is very limited in or near Langthwaite.

Calver Hill is an outstanding landmark in the dale. It looks down on both Swaledale and Arkengarthdale, and its curved summit and stepped profile make a distinctive shape that dominates the middle dale and invites further inspection. Sometimes called Calva Hill or Mount Calvey, the name could be of Biblical origin and is given as 'Calvary Hill' on a seventeenth century map. The religious connection has

been carried on by local people, who have had their ashes scattered on the top. One man went a step further and in 1937 had a large cross, made of rough limestone, built into the turf near the summit, now named after him as Gobat's Cross. The panorama from the top of Calver Hill is outstanding, but there is no right of way up to the trig point and walkers must be satisfied with a close view of it from all sides.

Langthwaite was the centre of the leadmining industry.

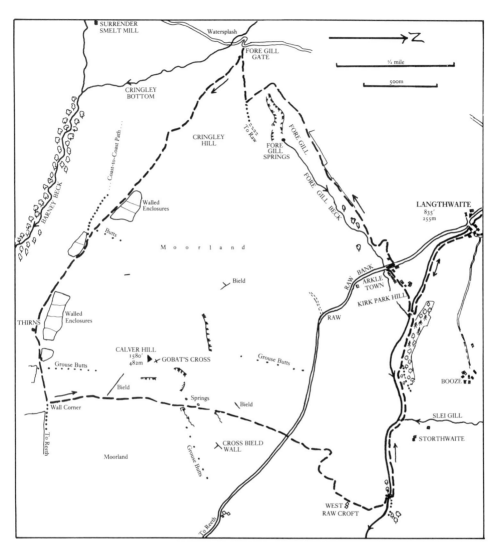

From the attractive little village of Langthwaite, take the path south along the left
bank of the Arkle, which begins opposite
the Red Lion Inn. The river may seem
peaceful enough, but a glance at the large
size of some of the boulders in its bed gives
some idea of the force of water needed to
move such objects. The dipper lives along
here and frequently perches on the

boulders as it bobs up and down, showing
off its white front bordered with chestnut.
The wren and the songthrush are two
musical residents, but you will also see the
colourful goldfinch and chaffinch.

Where the track leaves the riverside, turn
right over the wooden footbridge, right
again and up out of the narrow valley, and
across a field scattered with some quaint

75

old gravestones leaning in all directions. There is no sign of the parish church founded here at Arkle Town in 1145 and which in later centuries was allowed to deteriorate, possibly assisted by the strong Nonconformist element in Arkengarthdale. (The first Methodist chapel was built in 1798.) By 1818 the church was in such a poor state that it was dismantled and replaced by the one in Langthwaite. Arkle Town is now just a small, picturesque group of cottages.

Walk up through the hamlet to the road and turn right for a few paces to the field path signed 'Fore Gill Gate 1½ miles'. The path skirts Cumbers Hill with a number of interesting wild flowers along the way, including milkwort, tormentil, birdsfoot trefoil and lousewort. This last one likes the wetter places and the attractive purple flower was once thought to infest sheep with lice. However, in watery places, lousewort, like watercress, could aid the spread of liver-fluke to sheep via water snails. Cuckoo and meadow pipit are a likely 'pair' to be seen, the one laying its its egg in the other's nest. Fore Gill is a steep gorge dotted with clumps of trees and with a good miner's track leading to spoil heaps in the bottom of the gill. This might be the easiest route but the right of way stays above the gorge and is not well-defined.

Cross the gill at right angles through a wooden gate in the wall, and climb straight up to join a moorland track coming in from the left (from Raw near Arkle Town) and leading to Fore Gill Gate. The roadside here is a popular stopping place for motorists on their way from Arkengarthdale to Low Row. Many come to see the the watersplash, featured in the television film *All Creatures Great and Small.*

Turn your back to the gate and take the less well-worn, right fork of the two tracks, which leads south-east. On the immediate right is Blaeberry Gill leading to Cringley

Bottom, and on the left, the brow of Cringley Hill. Further to the right is a view of the Old Gang Valley, Surrender Bridge and a good length of Swaledale.

Calver Hill becomes more prominent on the left, and a line of grouse butts crosses the path. Near the corner of two fields, a path leads to the left over the shoulder of Calver. Keep above the fields through the heather and join the Coast-to-Coast route to the right of the next enclosures. Pass another line of stone grouse butts and, at the prominent wall corner on the right and by a small cairn, turn off to the left to continue on a green ribbon of turf through the heather with Fremington Edge to the right.

The path is good as far as the bield, now a broken wall, built in the last century as a sheep shelter. There are several such *bields* or shelters on the moor around Calver Hill, some being in the form of two walls joining each other in a T-shape.

The path continues under the impressive steep slopes and scars of Calver as far as a fenced spring below some old leadmine spoil heaps. By now you may have come across snipe, as this is a breeding area for them. A harsh call and a darting zigzag flight, as it hurries away, may be your first introduction to this interesting bird. It is present all year and nests in tussocks of grass in wet places. If you should get a close view of it, you will see the remarkably long bill which is about a quarter of the length of the bird. The tip of the bill is flexible which helps it to locate worms and other prey as it probes deep into wet ground.

From the spring there is no distinct path. Take a bearing by aiming at the distant stone towers (cairns) on the top left corner of Fremington Edge, or a little to the left of them. In mist or poor visibility, go 20° from north until you reach the road. The path goes between two bields, one of which is called Cross Bield Wall.

Cross the Arkengarthdale road, go down

The snipe uses its long bill to find to find food by probing deep into wet ground.

the winding track to West Raw Croft Farm and on down the lane to the footbridge over Arkle Beck. Turn left along the riverside field path. If you are not in a great hurry to complete the walk, there are some lovely flowers to look for along here. The built-up path leads through a wooden gate to a small footbridge and, yes, more spoil heaps! However, these are no eyesore and in fact would make a good picnic spot for the family.

In summer there is a lot of interest here for the botanist. There are flowers typical of limestone such as wood sage, scabious,

wild thyme, St John's-wort and rockrose. Mountain pansy and spring sandwort grow here too, and the purple and yellow of betony and lady's bedstraw add further colour.

Continue through the tunnel, a well-constructed example of leadminers' stonework, through the mixed wood with tall mature trees and join the track from Booze coming in from the right. Finally, pass by the footbridge you went over at the start of the walk and follow the river back into Langthwaite.

WALK 11: REETH, HEALAUGH AND SURRENDER BRIDGE

Start: Reeth. Grid Ref: 038 993
Distance: 7 miles (11km)
OS Maps: Outdoor Leisure 30 or Landranger 98 and 92
Walking Time: 3½ hours

There is great variety in this delightful walk, which begins along the banks of the Swale, continues by the woods of Barney Beck and returns on a stretch of moorland with wonderful views. The neat village of Healaugh and the fine ruins of Surrender smelt mill are visted on the way. The paths are distinct and undemanding except for the very steep descent at Cringley Bottom. Reeth is on the bus route from Richmond to Keld, and there is parking round the green.

Reeth, rather like Bainbridge and Kettlewell, was established as a forest edge settlement. The Old English meaning of the name, 'at the stream', is appropriate since Reeth is situated near the confluence of the River Swale and its most important tributary, Arkle Beck. Perched high above both rivers, the village occupies a fine vantage point on the hillside and its strategic position has, in modern times, earned it the title of the 'capital of Upper Swaledale'.

By the early nineteenth century, Reeth had become a thriving little town where a long history of leadmining had helped to expand the village and where hand-knitted stockings developed into an important trade. The miners and their families all took part in knitting, some gathering fallen wool, carding and spinning it in their homes. The small Swaledale Folk Museum throws interesting light on past activities of dalesfolk.

Today, Reeth attracts many visitors and makes an excellent starting place for some outstanding walks in the area. The river itself is of great interest to naturalists, while Harkerside, Calver Hill and Marrick Moor bring the moorland within easy reach. Marrick Priory and Fremington Edge are nearby, and the villages of Grinton and

Healaugh (where there are no car parks) are well worth visiting on foot.

Begin the walk by leaving the green in front of Barclays Bank and following the sign 'to the river', through the new bungalows. Turn right onto Quaker Lane and, instead of turning down to the river (*as in walk 6*), keep straight on 'to Healaugh' by a flower-lined sunken path. Notice the terraced strip lynchets of medieval farming. After passing through a flowery meadow, descend to the riverside. The banks of the river have been built up against flooding and are lined with alders, the roots of which help prevent erosion. A mile or so (2km) from Reeth, take the path to the right up to Healaugh.

Meaning a 'clearing in the forest', Healaugh (pronounced 'hee-law') was probably the furthest the Angles penetrated into Swaledale, leaving the upper part to the Vikings. The Anglian land passed to Walter de Gant, kinsman of William the Conquerer, when the Manor of Healaugh included all of Swaledale from Grinton to the source of the Swale and was largely a hunting forest, renowned for wolf and wild boar.

Harry Speight, writing about Swaledale in the 1890s, tells us that John o' Gaunt (son of Edward III), who was granted the

Honour of Knaresborough in 1372, came to his hunting lodge here with Thomas Chaucer, son of Geoffrey Chaucer of the *Canterbury Tales*. Thomas was Constable of Knaresborough and his wife a grand-daughter of the last heiress of the Manor of Healaugh.

At the time of the Dissolution the manor was owned by Sir Francis Bigod, who supported the old religion and became a leader of the Pilgrimage of Grace. By February 1537 he was captured and exe-cuted, along with Anthony Peacock of Arkengarthdale.

In 1556, half of the Manor of Healaugh was purchased by the powerful Wharton family. This gave them estates from Muker to Arkengarthdale where, over the next 100 years, they had a great influence on the dale and developed leadmining on a grand scale.

The village grew as a result of mining and also became a centre for dissenters. The Yorkshire Quaker, James Naylor, visited Healaugh in 1653 and meetings were held at Widow Longstaff's. Later a meeting house was built and used until about 1790. The Methodists lasted until 1983 when their chapel was closed. After the decline in leadmining, a hundred years ago, Harry Speight described Healaugh as 'neglected and in a tumble-down con-dition'. However, today it is a neat, compact and proud little village, sitting in a sheltered spot and facing the sun.

At the phone box, turn up to the right along a grassy, walled path with a stile at its end. Pass to the left of a barn and through flower-rich meadows where yellow rattle, red clover, buttercups and daisies grow. Yellow rattle (or hay rattle) is typical of old meadows and, when the seeds are ripe and rattle in their large seed boxes, then it is time to mow the hay.

Turn right onto a lane, lined on one side by limes, horse chestnut and beech trees, including a lovely copper beech. The

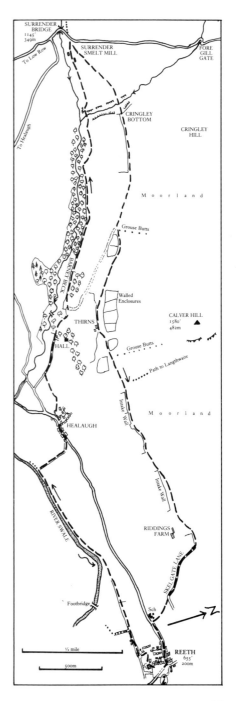

79

Harkerside from Reeth.

common lime is a hybrid between small-leaved and large-leaved lime. Its vigorous growth makes it the tallest broad-leaved tree in Britain and it often has sprouting branches near the base. In July the flowers of the lime tree can be collected and dried to make a sedative herbal tea. Place-names round here have a strange ring to them: Thiernswood Hall, Daggerstones Wood and Nova Scotia.

Pass Thiernswood Hall and enter mature woodland with tall trees of beech and pine. At the white gate, go through the stile and straight on but above the wood, returning to it again further on. Flowers growing in the wood are those most tolerant of shade, such as bluebells, wood sorrel and yellow pimpernel. The trees are a mixture of sycamore, birch, oak, pine and larch. It is a peaceful place, where you can hear the murmuring of Barney Beck deep down at the bottom of its V-shaped valley and find

pine cones with scales neatly bitten off by squirrels which collect the seeds.

Leave the wood and cross Bleaberry Gill. Climb up into moorland vegetation and to Surrender smelt mill. Named after the lead company, the ruined mill is in a fair state of preservation and is being partially restored. You can see the furnace where firebricks are coated with glassy slag, and the covered flue makes a long track up the hillside, where it used to carry fumes to a chimney. Built in 1839, the mill is in a prominent position and used to take ore from Surrender Mine at the top of Bleaberry Gill, as well as from Old Gang and other mines.

The road that crosses Surrender Bridge runs left to Healaugh and Feetham, and over to Arkengarthdale and Langthwaite to the right. Straight ahead, the continuation of Barney Beck is known as Old Gang Beck, and the track leads to Gunnerside

The white-fronted dipper is at home near fast-running water.

Gill via Old Gang smelt mill and mines. The short green turf by the beckside below the bridge makes a good picnic spot. This area is the haunt of the short-eared owl. On long silent wings, this beautiful bird glides close to the ground as it listens for the scuttling of a short-tailed vole or other small rodents. Since it hunts in daylight, it is more likely to be seen than other species of owl and worth looking out for.

From the bridge, double back above the mill on a moorland path to the deep ravine of Cringley Bottom. Ways down into the ravine of Bleaberry Gill are very steep and can be slippery. An easier descent is to the left of the steepest and now eroded tracks.

Wainwright, in his *Coast to Coast Walk*, suggests 'shuffling down on your bottom' as the safest method! The stile at the top of the far bank is near the wall corner.

Continue on a moorland path, first along the intake wall and then, keeping left of a double track, across open moor. There are magnificent views of the valley from this high-level path, with Calver Hill to the left. Pass a line of stone grouse butts, an area of mine tips and again take the route above the intake walls, above Riddings Farm, until you reach Skelgate Lane. The winding lane is an ancient routeway which takes you back to Reeth.

WALK 12: OLD GANG BECK AND REETH HIGH MOOR

Start: Surrender Bridge. Grid Ref: 989 999
Distance: 5½ miles (9km)
OS Maps: Outdoor Leisure 30 or Landranger 92 and 98
Walking Time: 3 hours

This moorland walk is much more interesting than it appears from the map, and can be accomplished in an afternoon or a summer's evening. The summit of Great Pinseat lies 220 yards (200m) from the path at an altitude of 915 feet (583m) above sea level. The total climb on the walk is only 770 feet (234m) and is managed in such a gentle gradient you hardly notice it. The paths are wide tracks all the way, so walking is easy, and the two main interests are moorland birds and leadmining. There is space for a few cars near Surrender Bridge, which lies on the minor roads from Healaugh and Feetham to Arkengarthdale, north of Langthwaite.

Surrender Bridge takes its name from the Surrender Mining Company, once owners of the smelt mill below the bridge and of Surrender Mine, high up on the moor near Great Pinseat. The area near the bridge is a good picnic place for motorists on their way to and from Arkengarthdale, and is the starting point for the walk onto Reeth High Moor.

Follow the Old Gang gravel track up the right side of the beck. It is a bridleway and popular for mountain bikers, so keep a look-out for them flying down the hill. The name Gang comes from Old English for road, so this is a very old routeway. The short-eared owl should be about, especially in the morning and evening. The valley of Old Gang Beck borders heather moors and you should also see meadow pipits and ring ouzels along here. The latter is typical of the rocky edges of the moors and very much a Swaledale bird. Known as the mountain blackbird, it arrives in March or April and in treeless areas nests on the ground or on a ledge of rock. Once you learn its shrill *pee-u* call, you may hear it before seeing it, the white crescent bib being its distinguishing mark.

Flowers alongside the track include spring sandwort, wild thyme, heath speed-well and heath bedstraw. Heath speedwell is a beautiful pale blue flower which likes dry places free of lime. Heath bedstraw forms a mat of white flowers and grows in a similar habitat. Mossy saxifrage is less common and is found by the beck; a plant of the uplands and rocky places, it has attractive white flowers that rise from mossy green leaves.

Arrive at Old Gang smelt mill, where there are lots of interesting things to look at and explore. There are ruins of the furnace house, several buildings and the black-smith's shop. At the back of the complex is a furnace arch and the base of a second arch, remains of an early mill which have been re-used as part of the flue system of a new mill. The half mile long (800m) flue up the hillside to the chimney on Healaugh Crag helped to increase the draught to the furnace and condense any remaining lead, which, as lead oxide, was scraped off the inside of the flue from time to time.

Built after 1828, the new mill is the large building parallel to the stream. At its peak the mill smelted 2,000 tons of lead a year. Inside it are the remains of machinery used to extract the mineral barite (a source of the metal barium) from the spoil heaps, in-stalled after lead smelting had ceased.

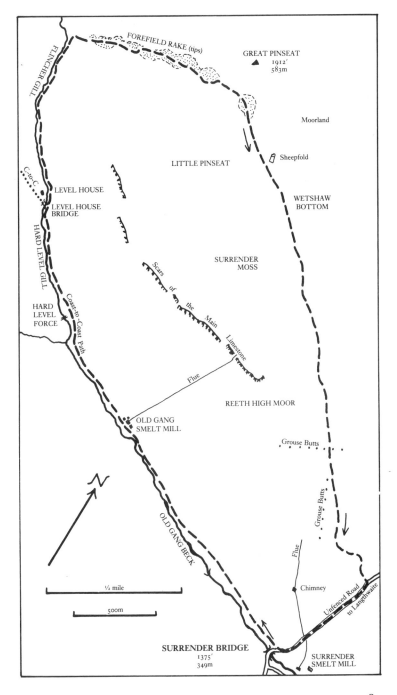

FOREFIELD RAKE (tips)

GREAT PINSEAT
▲ 1912'
583m

FLINCHER GILL

Moorland

LITTLE PINSEAT

Sheepfold

C-to-C

LEVEL HOUSE

LEVEL HOUSE
BRIDGE

WETSHAW
BOTTOM

HARD LEVEL GILL

SURRENDER
MOSS

Scars of the Main Limestone

HARD
LEVEL
FORCE

Coast-to-Coast Path

Flue

REETH HIGH MOOR

OLD GANG
SMELT MILL

Grouse Butts

Grouse Butts

N

OLD GANG BECK

Flue

Chimney

Unfenced Road to Langthwaite

½ mile

500m

SURRENDER BRIDGE
1375'
349m

SURRENDER
SMELT MILL

83

The remains of Old Gang smelt mill.

The peat house is still impressive, being 390 feet (119m) long. The rows of pillars mark the bays where peat was dried, and the whole building would have had a thatched roof. Enough peat could be stored here for a year's smelting at the mill.

Just above the mill is the entrance to the famous Hard Level, begun in 1780 by Lord Pomfret. It is estimated that the 1,100 yard (1km) tunnel must have taken fifteen years before striking Old Rake Vein to the north and linking a great complex of levels. It was continued as far again to Friarfold Vein. There is such a maze of tunnels that by the 1850s it was possible to go underground in Gunnerside Gill and, with one or two significant changes in level and a traverse of

six miles (8½ km) of passages, come out in Arkengarthdale!

Some 500 yards (450m) higher up the track is the attractive waterfall of Hard Level Force and, beyond the bridge, gravel is being reworked and a grouse track goes off to the right. On the far hillside, controlled heather burning in square plots has left a chequered pattern. Wheatear and pied wagtail are still to be seen along the beck, but look out for the timid snipe and more obvious curlew. If you think you hear the piercing song of a wren, you may not be mistaken for this tiny bird finds a home here even at 1,500 feet (450m) above sea level.

At Level House Bridge – a fine single

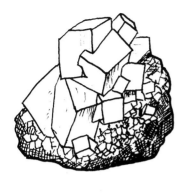

The 'gangue' minerals discarded by leadminers: fluorite and calcite (top), barite and witherite (below).

arch – take the right hand track alongside Flincher Gill. In the fork of the two tracks is the ruin of a stone building, Level House, once the home of Adam Barker, a lead-miner from Derbyshire whose name is remembered for three reasons. In 1676, he and his brother and the Quaker Philip Swale entered a partnership with Lord Wharton in a lease of Old Gang grounds, which brought in considerable income. After the Toleration Act of 1689, Adam's house was registered as a place for Non-conformist worship. His name also goes down in history for using a linen shroud for his daughter Ann's burial – her tomb is in Grinton Church – when wool was required by law, and Adam Barker was fined £5. In Charles II's time, this law was made to boost the woollen industry, but wealthy people would often pay the fine so that they could use the traditional linen.

Just above Level House Bridge are one or two large hushes, Old Rake Hush and North Rake Hush, carved out by repeated unleashing of water from dams to expose veins. Near the track is a shaly tip with ironstone nodules, containing pink and white dolomite, distinguished by its curved surfaces. The next tip contains bits of galena (the heavy grey ore of lead), sphaler-ite (the greasy brown-looking ore of zinc), barite (or barytes) which is heavy and white, and fluorite (or fluorspar) which has a more watery appearance. All of these minerals

85

can be seen in the track further on, which is surfaced with material from the tips. From the left, Doctor Gill joins Flincher Gill.

Cross the peat-stained stream and on to another area of pits and shafts. Bear right through a gateway and along the line of Forefield Rake, formerly a very rich vein. It is a scene of devastation, almost eerie with an atmosphere full of the ghosts of the leadmining industry. The track and tip are one and the same thing, and there are lots of beautiful pink pieces of barite about. A small pond lies to the left, and the lead-loving flowers of spring sandwort grow in healthy clumps here and there on the bare gravelly ground.

Arrive at the highest point of the walk where the path passes between two cairns built on tip heaps. Over to the left is a wall and the summit trig point of Great Pinseat at 1,912 feet (583m). There are some fine old bell pits here, and, among the rough heather and boggy ground, cloudberry grows, with its white flowers and bright green leaves.

This high part of the moor is good for birdwatching and you may have already heard the haunting call of the golden plover. They like the tussocky parts where they can take cover and, by July, start to gather in flocks. Snipe prefer the wetter ground and on a summer's evening you may hear them 'drumming' as the bird slides through the air, making its outer tail feathers vibrate in a throbbing sound. If you sit quietly, you may be rewarded by seeing a hen harrier gliding close to the ground in its search for prey. It will take almost anything from a large hare to voles, small birds, chicks, frogs and eggs. The male is a handsome pale grey with black wingtips, and the larger female (20 inches, 50cm) is streaky brown with a white rump. At the same time, keep an eye on the skies above for signs of the peregrine falcon which has quite a different hunting technique. High in the air, the peregrine may pause in its circling, fold back its wings and 'stoop' in a ferocious dive into the heather where a blow from the powerful talons knocks its prey senseless.

Proceed now in a south-easterly direction. The tips on the left are of Surrender Mine, the wet section of track is aptly named Wetshaw Bottom and Calver Hill is always in view ahead. Red grouse and meadow pipits are perhaps the two most common birds of the heather moors and are much in evidence. A plump grouse may make you jump as it explodes up in front of you out of the heather. The female, which is paler and a bit smaller than the male, lays up to a dozen eggs in a depression on the ground. They hatch after three weeks or so, and for two weeks the chicks run about among the heather until they can fly.

Further along, Swaledale comes into view and Arkengarthdale to the left. Pass some shooting butts, more tips and hushes and descend to the road, turning right to reach Surrender Bridge once more.

WALK 13: GUNNERSIDE, LOW ROW, HILL TOP AND BACK ALONG THE RIVER

Start: Gunnerside. Grid Ref: 951 982
Distance: 8 miles (13km)
OS Maps: Outdoor Leisure 30 or Landranger 98
Walking Time: 4 hours

A lovely mid-level walk along the south-facing slopes of the valley to Kearton returns along the riverside. The route passes through ancient Rowleth Wood, then the historic settlements of Smarber, Low Row and Kearton, dropping down to the river at Feetham Wood. The easy path along the riverbank via Isles Bridge is rich in flowers and birdlife. Gunnerside has a few places for cars in the village and by Gunnerside Bridge.

Gunnerside is a Viking name, meaning Gunnar's *saetr* (or summer pasture) and the original homestead may have been sited on the hillside above the present village. Harkerside, Ravenseat and Rogan's Seat are names of other summer pastures. Situated at the sheltered foot of the impressive ravine of Gunnerside Gill, Gunnerside became an important lead-mining centre. Its attractive, compact cluster of stone buildings were not only the homes of generations of leadminers but included the Kings Head (the Viking king, Gunnar, it is supposed), the smithy, literary institute and fine Methodist chapel. The walled fields round the village have shapes like crazy paving and are survivals of sixteenth century enclosures.

Take the road past the Kings Head and the post office and then, on the left, go steeply up through a gate. Leave the tarred road where it swings to the left and go straight ahead on a stony track. As you climb up the hill the path becomes grassy, and there is a view below of the fascinating tapestry of field barns and walls in Gunnerside Bottoms.

Continue up the walled green track, the old Corpse Road, along which the pall bearers carried the dead for burial at Grinton. Turn right over a step stile to pass

below Stanley Gill and Heights Farms, then along a string of stiles to enter Rowleth Wood. This is the most ancient patch of woodland in Swaledale and is exceptional in having aspects of a southern, lowland ash wood with the appearance of field maple (at the northern limit of its range), less rowan and more brambles and honeysuckle. Ash, sycamore and elm are the bigger trees, while blackthorn, bird cherry, ancient-looking hawthorns, holly and elder all grow together in a wild tangle. There are many damaged trees from the wet, heavy snow that fell in the winter of 1990, and fallen branches have been stripped of their bark by rabbits. Open glades afford views across the dale, and bluebells, primroses and wood sorrel brighten the sloping ground.

Songsters of the bird world include the resident blackbird and song thrush, the latter always repeating each phrase. In spring and summer you may hear the melodious tune of the blackcap and almost certainly that of the willow warbler, a most determined little bird that has survived a flight of 2,500 miles (4,000km) from tropical and southern Africa, its cheerful liquid song forming an easily-remembered cadence of descending notes. This warbler produces two broods in most seasons and,

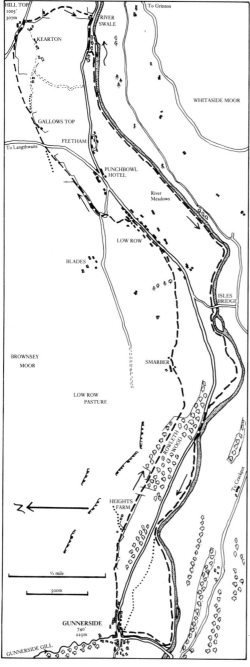

if you see the the young, they have a much more yellow appearance than the olive-brown adult.

Leave the wood and go through the fields to Smarber. This little place has some interesting history attached to it. Philip Lord Wharton, friend of Cromwell, was a Puritan sympathiser who made his shooting lodge at Smarber Hall available as a Nonconformist place of worship. By 1691 he had built a house alongside, as 'a public meeting house for protestants', which was used by the growing numbers of Con-gregationalists. About the same time, the seventy-seven year old Lord Wharton founded a charity to buy 1,050 Bibles every year for children who had learnt by heart seven specified psalms. The chapel was partly demolished in the nineteenth cen-tury, but there is a plaque which commem-orates 'the first independent chapel in Swaledale' and most families in the dale still have a 'Wharton Bible'.

Early Quakers also met in Smarber in a house near the chapel, which was held in trust as a meeting house and used until about 1730 when a new one was built at Low Row.

Go through Smarber farmyard and below the cottage on the wide downhill track to Low Row. Facing south on a lime-stone terrace, this linear village has some attractive cottages (one dated 1708) and larger houses facing a narrow green. The name comes from the fact that the original road along the dale ran higher up the hill-side through Blades and Barf. John Wesley was a visitor to Low Row and preached here in 1761. Blades and Low Row became meeting places for his followers and soon mid-Swaledale became a stronghold of Methodism. The village was also the home of Thomas Armstrong, author of the novel *Adam Brunskill*, a tale set among the leadminers of Swaledale.

Just along the road, in Feetham, is the

Above Gunnerside.

Punchbowl Hotel, formerly the Miners Arms, where funeral processions along the Corpse Road would come down for refreshment and a night's rest on their way to Grinton. The wicker coffin was left in the 'dead house', the foundations of which lie just above the village. Once, when two funeral parties were using the wayside mortuary at the same time, they found that, after the burial service and the effects of the refreshments had worn off, the bodies had been put in the wrong graves. Today the Punchbowl is a popular venue for mountain bikers and for cavers who explore the mines.

Keep above the road and below the cottages, then, just behind the assembly hall and before the church, turn up to the left. The path goes up by the graveyard and along to a minor road. After a few paces uphill, leave the road by going straight on at the hairpin bend along a flowery walled track where, in summer, rockrose, germander speedwell, lady's mantle, bugle, heath bedstraw and tormentil grow. Rockrose is particularly beautiful, having the most delicate of yellow petals, but the flower has no fragrance and no nectar.

The route reaches a more open landscape and crosses the road from Feetham to Arkengarthdale, where a sign indicates 'Hill Top 1¼'. The path leaves the farm track to the left and passes above the farms and the intake wall, a margin of moorland and home for lapwings and skylarks. Turn right at the road for 180 yards (200m), past the row of cottages known as Hill Top, to find the path down through the fields. The group of farms and cottages here make up the hamlet of Kearton, once a thriving community of large families. Park Hall and Healaugh Park, to the west, was a big house and estate, once owned by Philip, the fourth Lord Wharton.

Go steeply down through the fields to the left of the cottage and onto the road. Being watchful of traffic, turn right along the road for 320 yards (300m), then left through Feetham Wood to the riverside. In the wood grow kingcups, greater stitchwort, ground ivy, red campion and many more wild flowers.

Here begins three miles (5km) or so of delightful riverside walking, where you are likely to see pied and yellow wagtails, dipper, common sandpiper, redshank, oystercatcher and sand martin. Through binoculars, the brilliant canary colour of the yellow wagtail is astonishing when you first see it. This summer visitor can often be seen sitting on a fence and calling *tswee-ip* before moving on in undulating flight to another vantage point. The redshank is not numerous but its orange-red legs, loud

89

Cottages at Isles.

piping alarm call or the white trailing edges to its wings, when seen in flight, should distinguish it.

Some of the ungrazed meadows along the river contain a wealth of wild flowers. One of the first fields has the two primulas, cowslip and primrose, as well as the hybrid, false oxlip, which on one stem has a multiple head of large primrose flowers. In wet patches grow bright yellow kingcups, the nodding pinkish heads of water avens and, later in the summer, strongly-scented meadowsweet and yellow splashes of monkeyflower.

The riverbank has been built up against flooding and, after passing through a grove of mature larches, the path proceeds along the top of a substantial wall where large flagstones have fossil worm tracks snaking over the surface. The path emerges at Isles Bridge and the hamlet of Isles, where a big pebbly island in the river is the home of sandpipers and oystercatcher and, in summer, the tall yellow spikes of great mullein decorate the bank. A few years ago the river cut into its bank and formed a new channel, creating this island. If you wished to follow the right of way exactly then you would have to cross the river onto the island and back onto the bank again at the other end.

Further on, where river and road come close together, walkers are squeezed onto the road for 250 yards (230m) to rejoin the river for the rest of the walk. At Gunnerside Bridge, turn right through the fields alongside Gunnerside Beck and back into Gunnerside.

WALK 14: GUNNERSIDE GILL AND BLAKETHWAITE DAMS

Start: Gunnerside. Grid Ref: 951 982
Distance: 8 miles (13km)
OS Maps: Outdoor Leisure 30 or Landranger 98 and 92
Walking Time: 4 hours

This classic walk explores the full length of the dramatic gorge of Gunnerside Gill, first from the beckside and then returning on a higher level with views from above. The lower part of the gill is a prime area for flowers and woodland birds, the middle section a legacy of human endeavour in leadmining, and the narrow upper part takes you to the isolated Blakethwaite Dams and a taste of the open moor. There is limited parking in Gunnerside and by the bridge.

The fine, unspoilt stone village of Gunnerside is situated in the heart of upper Swaledale. It lies where the old route north of the river – the Corpse Road – and the main road merge for a short distance, and is divided by Gunnerside Beck which flows through the middle. The settlement on the east side of the stream formerly had the separate name of Lodge Green. The village has a pronounced character of its own, very much in the spirit of the dale. The large and impressive Methodist chapel, below the bridge, tells of a time when this was the centre for the followers of Wesley. The original chapel was built at a cost of £600 in 1789 – one of the earliest – and within six years had 100 members in Gunnerside. It was a period when the village was bound up with the fortunes of the leadmining industry. Many miners lived here and walked to work in the mines and mills, knitting as they went. In 1851, out of a population of 800, 180 worked in leadmining. Today the total population is about 200.

Cross the little bridge over Gunnerside Beck, dated 1911 and topped with red sandstone coping from the Eden Valley, and turn left up the right of the beck (opposite the Kings Head) on a streamside path lined with cow parsley and garlic mustard. These two white flowers are very common and easy to recognise. Drifts of cow parsley, or keck as it is known in Yorkshire, brighten up hundreds of miles of roadside verges in spring. The masses of delicate white flowers give it the descriptive name of Queen Anne's lace. Garlic mustard, or jack-by-the-hedge, is of the cabbage family with heart-shaped leaves which, when crushed, smell of garlic.

Go to the right, up steps past the old schoolhouse and, in spring or early summer, take time to look at some of the wild flowers along the way. Wet patches have marsh valerian, large bittercress, water avens and meadowsweet. Large bittercress is rather like a white version of lady's smock and grows by lime-rich streams. One or two good flowery banks on the right have primroses, violets, early purple and heath spotted orchids. In the more wooded parts grow bugle, wood sanicle, yellow pimpernel and toothwort. The last flower, seen in April or May, is interesting in that it has no green leaves; it is a creamy colour with pink petals and is parasitic on elm and hazel roots.

Where the path splits, keep to the lower route. Here in Birbeck Wood grow rowan, hazel, ash and bird cherry, all typical of northern ash woods. The bird cherry produces striking white blossom in May, though by July you may be able to recognise it by the festoon of silk webs after attack by

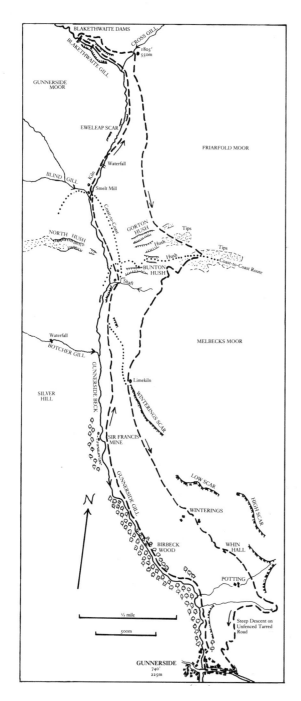

BLAKETHWAITE DAMS

CROSS GILL

BLAKETHWAITE GILL

1805'
550m

GUNNERSIDE
MOOR

EWELEAP SCAR

FRIARFOLD MOOR

BLIND GILL

Waterfall

Kiln

Smelt Mill

Coast-to-Coast

NORTH HUSH

GORTON
HUSH

Tips

Hush

Tips

Hush

Coast-to-Coast Route

BUNTON
HUSH

Shaft

Waterfall

MELBECKS MOOR

BOTCHER GILL

GUNNERSIDE BECK

Limekiln

SILVER
HILL

WINTERINGS SCAR

SIR FRANCIS
MINE

GUNNERSIDE GILL

LOW SCAR

HIGH SCAR

WINTERINGS

N

BIRBECK
WOOD

WHIN
HALL

POTTING

¼ mile

500m

Steep Descent on
Unfenced Tarred
Road

GUNNERSIDE
740'
225m

The bouse bays of Sir Francis Mine, used to store the untreated lead ore.

caterpillars of the bird cherry ermine moth.

The lovely stretch of steep woodland provides the walker with a view of the tree tops and a good chance to see some of the woodland birds. Apart from residents such as blackbird, tits and chaffinch, look out for the visiting pied flycatcher. The male is a handsome black and white, and both adults have the habit of swooping on the wing for insects. The bird is the size of a robin, but the wings, eyes and tail are somewhat larger – all the better to catch flies with.

Leave the woods behind and descend onto a flat grassy 'plain' where you may see the yellow, upward-looking faces of mountain pansies and the tiny white stars of spring sandwort.

The first spoil heaps are just ahead where the crushing mill was located. Across the gill is the rusty cylinder of a compressed air chamber that helped to speed up the driving of the level of Sir Francis Mine, the entrance to which is below. The level was cut to drain water from below the mines

along the complex of veins 1,500 yards (1.4km) to the north, to tap any deeper veins and to assist in haulage of ore from the mines. Started in 1864, the first 404 yards (370m) took five years and cost £2,000. Then rock drills powered by compressed air were introduced and, in 1873, the use of dynamite speeded up things considerably. By 1877 the level hit the rich Friarfold vein. A new shaft was made and a hydraulic pumping and winding engine installed, the remains of which are still underground. The mine became highly mechanised and profits came in which, today, would be measured in millions of pounds. The mine closed in 1882 when cheap imported ore caused prices to slump.

Continue up the hill, past Botcher Gill Nook on the left; Dolly Mine is also seen on the far side of the valley. Almost on the track itself is Bunton Mine and dressing floor. The ruined buildings include the offices, stables and blacksmith's shop. The seventeen bay bouse store and waterwheel pit are easily picked out. Bouse is the miner's term for the ore plus other minerals that came straight from the mine, before it was concentrated by hammering or crushing. Bunton Mine and Lownathwaite Mine, across the valley, both tapped the Friarfold vein complex and the richest ore in Swaledale. The entrance to the Bunton Level is at the foot of Bunton Hush and, just beyond the bluff on the hillside, is the Underset limestone in Friarfold Hush.

In the seventeenth century, mining was done by hushing, whereby a flood of water was released to scour the top of the mineral vein and expose more ore. The enormous gullies on both sides of Gunnerside Gill are the result of repeated hushing. They were a devastating alteration to the landscape and now appear as incredible monuments to man's ingenuity. The National Park, with two other bodies, are planning ways to conserve them.

The landscape of Gunnerside Gill has been greatly affected by man's incessant search for lead.

From the vantage point of Bunton Mine, look out for ring ouzels. This is a favourite place for these summer visitors, which replace the blackbird in these higher, wilder parts. They like the steep rocky outcrops and slopes, and you may hear either the chatting alarm call or the more appealing *pee-u*. They also have a shrill piping song of three or four notes: *pee-pirri-pee*.

Descend to the beck and, in a third of a mile (500m) from Bunton Mine, arrive at the impressive ruins of the Blakethwaite peat store and smelt mill at the junction with Blind Gill. The mill furnace was within the cast iron pillars which supported arches, behind which flues carried the smoke and fumes steeply up the cliffs at the back of the mill to a small chimney 150 feet (45m) above. Blakethwaite Mine was in use in the early nineteenth century.

Continue up the beck to cross over at the next lot of ruins by a pretty waterfall, and follow up the narrow ravine past Eweleap Scar where heather moor descends to stream level. Cross the side stream of Cross Gill by a sheep fold where wild thyme and mossy saxifrage grow on limestone. There are two Blakethwaite dams, long disused. The first one is broken and there is not much to show for it. However, the upper one has a fine water race built of large blocks of millstone grit, though the reservoir above is silted up.

Turning acutely to the right, make for the track and shooting box near the end of a line of grouse butts. From the shooting box (of Lord Peel's estate) there is a fine view of the gill. Continue on the made-up vehicle track to the high point at 1,800 feet (550m) above sea level. Pass the sign to Keld, then turn away from the gill to a cairn which declares '100 miles' for the Coast-to-Coasters. The view east of Merry Field is one of mine tips and desolation. It is said that the Merry Field vein was so rich that as much ore was extracted as spoil. It makes you think, since there are spoil heaps as far as the eye can see!

Turn sharp right through this moonscape to another cairn and along down the gill again. The surfaced track ends but continues as a grassy path with hairpin bends. The path crosses Swina Bank and at Winterings Scar joins the path that comes up from the gill. Here is a fine limekiln where limestone was burnt for lime, which was spread on the land to make it more fertile. Some lime was also used to make mortar for building.

Carry on along the track to Winterings and Whin Hall to a fork. Take the right hand one and immediately go through a wooden gate onto a tarred road which winds steeply down back to Gunnerside. On the way there are wonderful views of Gunnerside and Swaledale.

WALK 15: IVELET MOOR FROM GUNNERSIDE

Start: Gunnerside. Grid Ref: 951 982
Distance: 8 miles (13km)
OS Maps: Outdoor Leisure 30 or Landranger 98 and 92
Walking Time: 4 hours

This wonderful high-level circuit of Ivelet Moor has superb views over Swaledale, Kisdon Gorge, Swinner Gill and Gunnerside Gill. The walk follows the steep edge of these grouse moors, crossing them on the northern leg, where a height of 1,900 feet (980m) is reached. Beyond Ivelet the path is not so easy to follow, but from Swinner Gill there is a good track all the way. The main attractions are the views, prehistory and grouse moors. Parking is limited to a few spaces by Gunnerside Bridge and in the village.

Pause a while in Gunnerside and consider what it may have been like when, for 300 years, leadmining dominated the lives of the inhabitants. The biggest boom came between about 1780 and 1820, but much lead was mined up to the 1880s when the real slump brought misery and migration. Large families lived in small cottages, two of which have been combined to make a reasonably-sized modern home. Wages varied with profits but conditions in the mines were dreadful. Life expectancy was low. In 1860, the average age of death for miners was only 46, but for non-miners it was 61. There were accidents in the mines, but most men died from chest diseases through breathing dust. Damaged lungs led to tuberculosis in many, and others suffered from lead poisoning.

The final decline in leadmining caused a large number of people in the village to leave and find work elsewhere. James Reynoldson, who left to work in the Lancashire cotton mills, wrote two hymns, one called *Gunnerside* and the other *Muker*, which were sung regularly in the Wesleyan chapels of the dale.

The old inn sign of the King's Head was said to have a close resemblance to the landlord, but the present one reverts to the head of a Viking, proclaiming that Gunnar

once ruled here. On the other side of the beck, the nineteenth century literary institute is a landmark to an intelligent people, eager for learning and self-improvement. It is here that the Gunnerside brass band played regularly. It was one of the earliest in the dale and, in 1832, they marched over Oxnop Gill to play in Askrigg on polling day. Soon most villages had a brass or silver band, including Keld, Angram, Thwaite and Muker.

Beginning the walk from the Kings Head, go over the bridge and straight ahead between the cottages, old and new, which leads through the meadows to Ivelet. June is the best time to see the colourful hay meadows where, among the flowers, grow yellow rattle, cat's ear (a yellow hawkbit), red clover, yarrow and meadow cranesbill.

When the river comes into view, keep to the right, above the riverbank. After a couple of fields, pass a barn with fine roofed doorways. On the other side of the river is the small hamlet of Satron. Squeeze through one or two tight stiles to cross a footbridge over the wooded Shore Gill and enter Ivelet, a small, peaceful group of stone cottages. Ivelet is best known for its elegant packhorse bridge. (*See walk 16*.)

Turn up the road, past Gunnerside Lodge, the home of the local landowner,

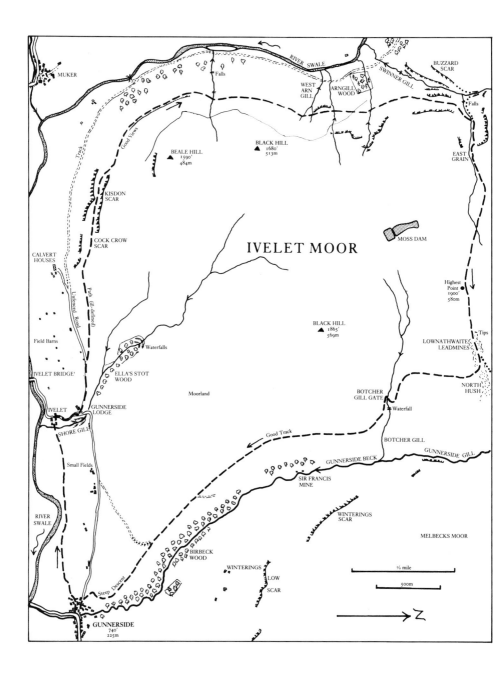

MUKER

RIVER SWALE

Falls

BUZZARD
SCAR

SWINNER GILL

WEST
ARN
GILL

ARNGILL
WOOD

Falls

EAST
GRAIN

BEALE HILL
1590'
484m

BLACK HILL
1680'
513m

KISDON
SCAR

COCK CROW
SCAR

CALVERT
HOUSES

IVELET MOOR

MOSS DAM

Highest
Point
1900'
580m

Field Barns

Waterfalls

Tips

LOWNATHWAITE
LEADMINES

BLACK HILL
1865'
569m

IVELET BRIDGE'

ELLA'S STOT
WOOD

Moorland

BOTCHER
GILL GATE

NORTH
HUSH

IVELET

GUNNERSIDE
LODGE

Waterfall

SHORE GILL

Good Track

BOTCHER GILL

Small Fields

GUNNERSIDE BECK

GUNNERSIDE GILL

SIR FRANCIS
MINE

RIVER
SWALE

BIRBECK
WOOD

WINTERINGS
SCAR

MELBECKS MOOR

WINTERINGS

LOW

SCAR

½ mile

500m

Steep Descent

N

GUNNERSIDE
740'
225m

Earl Peel, and left at the top along an unfenced stretch of byroad with exceptional views down the dale and across to Oxnop Gill.

Near the brow of the hill, 500 yards (450m) from the village, leave the road for the footpath on the right (not the grouse road). There is no worn path, so follow the reed-filled ditch and aim above the notch on the horizon which is Cock Crow Scar. Just above this point, about 100 yards (90m) to the right, are some Romano-British field patterns.

Continue below Kisdon Scar, the high limestone scars on the right, and follow the short, green turf along a shelf of land between two scars. Here you have a glorious view of Swaledale, Muker, Kisdon Hill and Great Shunner Fell.

Keep up above the sloping ground which steepens and becomes the limestone scar of Ivelet Boards. As you curve round along this scar, you obtain a magnificent view of the Swale, 550 feet (170m) below, in beautiful Kisdon Gorge with the ruined Crackpot Hall at the head of the valley.

Cross Arn Gill, where ash and birch take shelter and green-veined white butterflies visit marsh thistles, and keep well up the valley slope, above Arn Gill Scar. It was here, about seventy years ago, that a game-keeper, John Cherry of Muker, lost his ferret in the screes at the foot of the scar. He pulled out a lot of rocks and found a pile of human bones. More recently, the Natural History Museum has dated the remains of this skeleton as between 2,000 and 3,000 years old – that is, from the Bronze Age period. It was a chance find, but of great importance to the prehistory of Swaledale.

Cross West Arn Gill, after which descend a little and join a worn path, cross another gill and then a wall by gate or ladder stile. (This wall has been occasionally in view well up to the right, since Cock

Crow Scar.) Wind up through the bracken above Arngill Wood. On a small ledge to the right there are some hut circles, one of which is in a small enclosure, tucked under the overhanging scar. It is a small Iron Age settlement.

Here the route enters the beautiful enclave of Swinner Gill. Deep below, the beck tumbles over several falls to reach the Swale near Arngill Wood. The Yoredale limestones form scars, one above the other on the valley side, and it is here that the ring ouzel and wheatear return each spring.

The path crosses the beck of East Grain and turns up the hill, away from Swinner Gill, to the moor above. Near where the path crosses the stream, look for New Zealand willowherb, a diminutive trailing plant with tiny white flowers on long, bare, brown stems. The plant was introduced from New Zealand for use in rock gardens, the first escape being noted in 1908. It has spread rapidly since then and grows in wet, stony places by upland streams, where there is little competition from other plants.

As you climb up East Grain, notice, on the uneven ground, the tufa blocks near the path. Tufa is a spongy-looking rock, originally deposited as calcium carbonate on moss or peat by water that came down through the limestone. It is common around springs in limestone country.

The next mile (1,600m) is part of the Coast-to-Coast footpath and is well signposted before it joins Earl Peel's new grouse track. Over to the right is the double tarn of Moss Dam, a breeding place for black-headed gulls and, as you gain height, there are views of Great Whernside and Buckden Pike in Wharfedale, of Penyghent and Ingleborough and, nearer by, Lovely Seat and Great Shunner Fell. On a clear day, from the highest point on the walk at 1,900 feet (580m), the distant mountains are spectacular.

The walk passes by grouse butts and

North Hush, leading into Gunnerside Gill. Hushes were artificial gullies which were flooded to remove the topsoil and expose the veins of lead ore.

Meadow cranesbill is so common throughout the dale that it often fills the roadside verges.

large areas of heather moor. The main use of the land is for grouse shooting, which is usually confined to a short season of about three months from the 12th August. The red grouse is classed as a 'race' of the more widespread willow grouse, but is never-theless an exclusively British bird. It is territorial, staying close to its breeding area all year. The hawking and netting of grouse on the Swaledale moors was a sport of the gentry for centuries, and was largely re-placed by the shotgun 150 years ago. The keeping of grouse requires management of the heather, which is burned every few years in small plots, so that birds may have cover in mature heather but are also able to feed on the succulent young shoots of the new growth. Such management has in-cluded the persecution of merlin, peregrine and hen harrier, though all three survive in a small way. On the other hand, golden plover, curlew and lapwing, as well as skylark and meadow pipit, have had fewer predators and so have done well.

Pass the amazingly deep, leadminer-made gully of North Hush to the left and, leaving the Coast-to-Coast route, curve round to the right and on to Botcher Gill Gate. The gill is a narrow ravine with a waterfall and a fine view down into Gun-nerside Gill. Further on, the track over-looks the gill with a view of the bouse store of Sir Francis Mine. On the hillside above the path grow the light and feathery wood horsetail and, along the way, you may catch sight of one or two partridge, showing an orange-brown tail when in flight.

Where the track swings round to the right, leave it for a grassy path down the hillside towards Gunnerside. The path emerges via a gated stile opposite the village institute.

99

WALK 16: MUKER, IVELET BRIDGE AND OXNOP GILL

Start: Muker. Grid Ref: 910 979
Distance: 5½ miles (9km)
OS Maps: Outdoor Leisure 30 or Landranger 98
Walking Time: 2½ hours

This lovely walk begins with a pleasant stroll through riverside meadows in a beautiful part of upper Swaledale, visits the most graceful bridge over the Swale, continues for a short excursion into Oxnop Gill and returns through the fields to Muker. It is good for flowers and river birds. There is a car park by the bridge in Muker.

The most picturesque of Swaledale's villages, Muker lies in a wonderful setting amid the most beautiful and unspoilt part of the dale. The village has changed little over the years, and looks very like the photograph in Harry Speight's book of 1896, with the stone bridge over Muker Beck, a collection of houses and cottages arranged on the hillside, and the church and clocktower rising above them all. It is the main village of the upper end of the dale, and 150 years ago it had a population of 1,300 people, three times the present number. The original church was dedicated in 1580, a rare Elizabethan example, thatched with heather and floored with rushes in those days. Restored in 1890, when the musicians' gallery was removed and a new, higher roof made, it still fits in perfectly with its surroundings.

Muker School was founded in 1687 and its most famous students, who attended in the nineteenth century, were the brothers Richard and Cherry Kearton. It was the love of nature in their native Swaledale that led them to become pioneers in wildlife photography, naturalists, writers and exploreres. Two plaques on the wall of the old school, now a craft shop, commemorate them. Next door, the woollens shop was the schoolmaster's house with a door to the schoolyard. The graceful Victorian building of the literary institute stands out

among the stone cottages. In the 1890s it had a reading room and library of 600 books, and has been the meeting place for lectures, band concerts, Women's Institute activities, evening classes and dances ever since. The silver band still plays and has been the most successful of the village bands.

The village store stocks every kind of necessity, as well as being a tea shop and National Park information point. The pub is the Farmers Arms and the post office is on the hill. There is even a small green.

Begin by going up the hill into the village and round the right side of the post office, taking the footpath through the fields labelled 'Keld and Gunnerside'. Hay meadows are spectacular in the early summer, and those near Muker are some of the finest in the Dales and of high botanical value. First they turn yellow with buttercups and yellow rattle, then white with pignut; splashes of purple and red are provided by wood cranesbill and red clover. Look out for the tall, reddish-purple melancholy thistle, with its large and beautiful single flower-heads. The buds of this thistle with no prickles may droop to give the plant a sad appearance, but its name comes from its supposed ability to cure the mental state of melancholia.

On reaching the River Swale, turn right and cross the footbridge, a solid structure with a large central stone pillar and a view upstream into the majestic Kisdon Gorge. Turn right again down the left bank, signed 'Gunnerside'. (To arrive at Ramps Holme, it looks possible from the OS map to cross the river in an alternative short-cut from Muker, worth trying if the river is very low, but there are no stepping stones so you could get your feet wet.)

Fork right on a lower path ('via Ivelet') to stay on the riverside through more colourful meadows with scattered barns. This is good farmland, developed on river alluvium, deposited where Muker Beck joins the Swale – the name Muker comes from Norse for meadow. A striking part of the rural scene is the number of field barns and cow byres. Few are now used in the old way, but they used to house three or four cows through the winter which were fed on hay, stored above them. If you see one with a fresh muck heap outside, then it is a rare example of traditional use.

Yelland's Meadow is a field across the river, owned by the Yorkshire Wildlife Trust. It is the first Dales hay meadow to be made a nature reserve and is farmed in the traditional way by a local farmer. The three acre field (1.2ha) includes a barn, a small stream through the middle and a wide variety of flowering plants.

From the second week in April, listen for the piping notes of the sandpiper which returns from Africa to take up residence along the river. The musical call of this small but attractive wader signals the coming of warmer weather. Another river bird, best seen in the winter, is the brilliantly-coloured, though shy, kingfisher. You may hear its shrill call, but if you see it flash by, watch where it lands, to get a rare close view.

There are some newly-planted trees, and in places the riverbank has been neatly reinforced, but now the roots of alder and sycamore guard the bank from erosion.

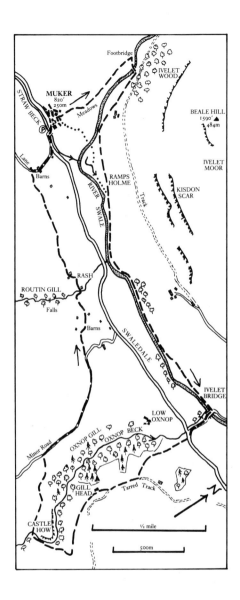

Arrive at Ivelet Bridge, a beautiful single arch across the river and the finest bridge in Swaledale. Its high hump-back is wide enough for one car, but the crest is so sharp that a driver could be forgiven for thinking his vehicle might be marooned with all four

The fine packhorse bridge at Ivelet is one of the gems of the dale.

wheels in the air. It is a fine packhorse bridge built to link the old road up the dale with the route over Oxnop to Askrigg in Wensleydale. It is not shown on Jeffreys' map of 1771 and its age is uncertain, though Geoffrey Wright puts it at about 1690. This quiet, tree-shaded spot is haunted by a headless black dog and, if you should see it, tragic consequences will follow.

Cross Ivelet Bridge, go up the lane and then across the main road to climb up fields on the left side of Oxnop Gill. A stile at the top of the field with a barn in the middle of it takes you onto a tarred byroad. (The higher part of the gill is also worth exploring where the small road goes above Oxnop Scar. It is a high, airy walk that provides some lovely views.)

After 220 yards (200m), turn off to the right in front of Gill Head Farm. Follow the wall and cross a stile, on the left of a gate gap, by a tall ash tree. Follow the contour above Oxnop Gill and cross a

Looking down the upper dale towards Muker.

limestone boulder-strewn hollow, the dry valley of Spout Gill. A stile near the upper end of the wood takes you along the edge of a wooded ravine, with Oxnop Beck in the bottom. Trees include a mixture of bird cherry, hazel, birch, rowan, willow and ash, and give good cover for redstart and other woodland birds.

Descend to a wooden footbridge and follow the waymarks through fields to the Swaledale to Askrigg road. The roadside verge is a haven for flowers, including lady's mantle, water avens and common valerian; the latter is tall and has a dense flower-head of a pale pinkish colour.

Turn left off the road at the hairpin bend, through sloping fields, keeping along the contour. Pass through the community of Rash and along a steep hillside scattered with holly and hawthorns. Just before Muker, turn right on a green lane and return to the start of the walk. The picture postcard view of Muker is from this lane just before the bridge.

WALK 17: MUKER, KISDON GORGE AND SWINNER GILL

Start: Muker. Grid Ref: 910 979
Distance: 6½ miles (10½km)
OS Maps: Outdoor Leisure 30 or Landranger 98 and 92
Walking Time: 3½ hours

This is the most spectacular walk in the dale, a real favourite. Starting at Muker, it follows the Swale through Kisdon Gorge, part of Swaledale with no road and no traffic. It visits the two attractive water-falls of Kisdon Force and East Gill Falls, climbs to the ruins and scenic viewpoint of Crackpot Hall, and continues into the dramatic ravine of Swinner Gill, with an easy walk back along the riverside. All in all, it is a classic. There is a car park at Muker.

The pretty village of Muker lies in the heart of unspoilt countryside. The name means 'meadow' and round about are some of the best flower-rich meadows in the Dales. The field barns and byres are also a feature of the area, there being sixty-three barns within 1,100 yards (1km) of Muker. But Muker grew, like other Swaledale villages, with the leadmining industry and many of the cottages were the homes of miners.

Many visitors congregate here. It is the most attractive village in the dale, with a growing number of services which include a small car park (hidden across the beck), an excellent village store and tea shop, a gift shop and gallery, a post office and Swale-dale Woollens – a cottage shop dealing in sweaters knitted in the dale and made from local wool. There is a guesthouse, the pub is the Farmers Arms and the National Park information point is in the village store, where books and maps are available. The surrounding countryside is a walker's paradise where, within only three miles (5km) of the village, there are forty miles (64km) of public rights of way.

Go up into the village and take the path to the right of the post office which leads through meadows to the banks of the Swale. These few fields are typical of the northern, wood cranesbill meadows. The

tall, strong plant of wood cranesbill is common, responds well to traditional management and likes the cool, wet climate of the Dales. Melancholy thistle is another northern species which appears just here and there, and other flowers include meadow vetchling, rough hawkbit, tufted vetch and harebell.

On reaching the river, continue up the left side with Kisdon to the left and Ivelet Moor to the right. This beautiful valley, known as Kisdon Gorge, can only be fully explored by the walker. It was formed by torrents of water from melting glacier ice, some 13,000 to 14,000 years ago, when the former path of the Swale to the west of Kisdon was blocked by boulder clay. The fast-flowing river cut deeply into the land, making the narrow gorge at Keld and producing this broad, secluded valley.

The path along the river terrace descends to the river level and a very pleasant walk follows, on short turf. Look out for the stoat along here, which may run in and out of the broken wall, hunting for mice or young rabbits. You may be able to attract its attention by giving a high-pitched squeak like a frightened animal. There is a fine view of Swinner Gill and Crackpot Hall ahead. At Hartlakes there was once the cottage of a coalminer who worked at Tan Hill. He would ride to work on a donkey

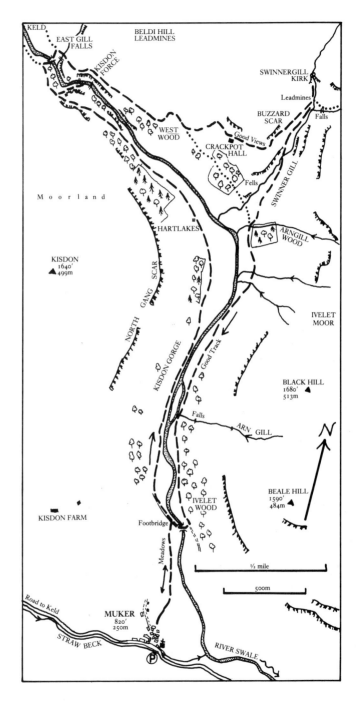

Swinner Gill from Hartlakes, in Kisdon Gorge.

cart and, in the evening, fill it with coal to sell on the way home. The cottage is known as 'Boggle House' and, although used as a shelter for many years, it is avoided on dark nights because it is haunted.

Climb up and enter a wooded section with ash, birch and alder. Birds include nuthatch and redstart. Pass a small limekiln on the right, join the Pennine Way by a limestone scar, where yew trees and hare-bells grow, and take the short path to see the splendid double falls of Kisdon Force and the deep rocky gorge into which they pour. The little path passes under Birk Hill, where a large pinacle of rock has become detatched from the face of the scar.

There is a good assortment of flowers on the limestone.

Retreat to the main path and, 100 yards (90m) further along, branch down to the right to the new wooden footbridge over the Swale. Just to the right of the bridge on the near side is a fine head-on view of the attractive East Gill Falls, where the beck descends in three steps to join the Swale. Until 1899 there stood a graceful pack-horse bridge here over the river, but it was destroyed in the flood of that year.

Cross the footbridge, where you can inspect the waterfalls of East Gill more closely, and climb up to join the Coast-to-Coast route on a wide track. Turn right

Crackpot Hall was occupied as recently as the 1950s.

through a gate, above the falls, for a lovely path that takes you high above the gorge. It turns up to the left and crosses Old Field Hush. This was worked from 1738 until 1846, and was the scene of much inter-company quarrelling between the Parkes brothers' company of Beldi Hill Mines and that of Lord Pomfret whose mines were in Swinner Gill.

The rivalry started about 1750 when the Parkes walled up a level which served both mines and, by diverting a stream from the moor, flooded part of Lord Pomfret's mine. In 1767, the dispute took a new turn. Till then the land of Out Hall Pasture was considered part of Crackpot Farm, owned by Thomas Smith, and mining dues were paid to him. However, after huge profits were made from mines on Out Hall, Lord Pomfret claimed that this land was part of the Manor of Muker and belonged to him. The resulting lawsuit was eventually won by Smith, who received £400 compensation. But Lord Pomfret, in debt because of the many trials, was imprisoned in the Tower of London.

During the trials, miners of both parties were active in support of their companies. Attempts were made to flood rivals' mines, and when David Brunskill tried to prevent the flooding of a shaft on Beldi Hill, he was thrown into Hush Gutter, the stream that flows down through Old Field Hush.

In 1846, with twenty men, James Kearton reworked Old Field Hush. Two dams were made above the hush and a grated pit was dug in the bed of it to trap the ore. The two dams were different distances from the top of the hush so, when they were released, complex signals were made so that the torrents of water reached the top of the hush at the same time. The ore, having been loosened with picks, was swept down and caught in the pit. A tramway carried the ore to the dressing floors and then to the smelt mill. Arthur Raistrick tells us that the hush was worked in this way for sixteen years and was very productive.

Fork left near the rusting hulk of an old Ferguson tractor and reach Crackpot Hall. Behind the ruined buildings are the remains of the crushing mill, where a large wheel pit can still be seen. (The smelt mill is at the foot of Swinner Gill.) The old farmhouse of Crackpot Hall was built by Lord Wharton for his keeper, who looked after the red deer that roamed the wooded hillsides of the seventeenth century. It was occupied until the 1950s but, due to mining subsidence, has gradually collapsed. The view from here is one of the finest in the dale as it looks right down Kisdon Gorge to Muker.

Continue up the track, above the hall, and past buildings of the former smithy. After further exhilarating views down the valley, the path becomes narrow and rocky as it turns under the sandstone outcrops of Buzzard Scar and into the scenic gorge of Swinner Gill. At the head of the gill and at the junction with Grain Gill is a fine stone bridge, a waterfall and a mine entrance. Here, on the east of the gill, are Swinner-gill Mines, with dressing floors and the ruins of a smelt mill.

To visit Swinnergill Kirk, scramble upstream into a narrow gorge where the strata dips sharply into the gill, emphasising its depth, and where limestone slabs are sculptured and pitted by the dissolving action of peaty water. By the splashing water of Swinnergill Falls is the cave of Swinnergill Kirk where, in times of religious intolerance (the 1670s and 80s), dissenters came and held services in secret. The damp atmosphere and the wet rocks and ledges are home to New Zealand willowherb, herb robert, wood sorrel and primroses, but also the pretty ferns of maidenhair and green spleenwort, brittle bladder fern, as well as mosses and liverworts.

Between the kirk and the bridge there is the beginning of an interesting series of Yoredale strata. Below the limestone, near the cave, is sandstone, then black shale. Then comes another layer of limestone with its own little gorge just where the main track crosses the beck by the bridge. The view from here is awesome, more a peephole than a panorama as it looks right down Swinner Gill and the length of Kisdon Gorge beyond.

From here the route continues on a narrow path down the right bank of Swinner Gill, crossing to the other side about halfway down the narrow ravine. The scenery is as dramatic as anywhere in the Dales and, as care is needed on the steep slopes, it is exciting in more ways than one. Further outcrops of limestone, sandstone and shale are well exposed in the side of the gill, one below the other. Where the path descends to stream level, some sandstone contains black (carbonaceous) plant remains and black shale forms the bank. It is a sheltered spot, and near the beck a mine level gushes with clear water.

Cross the beck above a small waterfall and proceed high on the left bank. Another limestone (the fourth) can be seen, forming a waterfall; then a fifth, the Underset limestone, outcrops at the foot of the gill. The ruins of Beldi Hill smelt mill, built in 1771, stand near the junction of the beck with the Swale.

Below Arngill Wood, join the delightful wide track alongside the River Swale. One mile (1.6km) further on, cross the river by the footbridge and join the path through the meadows back to Muker.

WALK 18: KISDON, KELD AND THWAITE FROM MUKER

Start: Muker. Grid Ref: 910 979
Distance: 7 miles (11km)
OS Maps: Outdoor Leisure 30 or Landranger 98 and 92
Walking Time: 3½ hours

This splendid, classic walk combines glorious views from Kisdon Hill, a stretch of the Corpse Road, a visit to the three delightful villages at the top of the dale and two picturesque waterfalls. The walk can be started from Keld or from Thwaite, and the triangle of Muker, Kisdon Farm and Thwaite makes a beautiful shortened walk, perfect on a summer's evening. There is a small car park at Muker.

Muker, like other villages in the upper part of Swaledale, was founded by Norse Vikings, whose names of landmarks and homesteads still survive, along with many dialect words. Muker means a narrow field, Keld a spring and Thwaite a clearing. In his fascinating book *Muker, The Story of a Yorkshire Parish*, Edmund Cooper tells us of the outstanding characters and families, and of the hardships and festivities of the hard-working and determined inhabitants. About 1560, local people took successful action against the new lord of the manor, Lord Wharton, to safeguard their tenant rights, when eighty-nine year old Edward Milner of Muker was among the yeomen who gave evidence. Times were hard and, in the 1780s, over a third of the Muker burials were recorded as paupers, mostly miners or their wives and children. Paupers had no legal rights and were entitled to get relief only from the parish in which they were born.

But there were good times, and the Christmas feast, known as Muker Awd Roy, was a four day affair starting on the 6th January (a survival of the ancient feast of Epiphany). Work was suspended in the leadmines, wives baked cheesecakes, Christmas loaves and 'secret-cakes', stalls were set up in the market place, a day was reserved for outdoor sports, the silver band had its busiest time and the three Muker

inns became centres of merrymaking where fiddlers played to singing and dancing.

Start by going up into Muker village, to the left of the post office and up a lane, soon to turn off to the left and zigzag up the hill on a partly-tarred track. Stay on this, aiming for a lone farmhouse with a barn at each end. Turn right onto the Pennine Way, a path which runs high on the side of Kisdon Gorge, with magnificent views across to Ivelet Moor and ahead to Swinner Gill with the ruins of Crackpot Hall looking down the dale.

The scars above the path are North Gang Scar, outcrops of the Main limestone, and contain the large fossil lampshell *Gigantoproductus*. Common whitlow grass grows among the rocks, its tiny white flowers showing very early in the spring. The larger, fleshy-leaved scurvygrass also grows here and flowers through the summer. The leaves contain vitamin C and were eaten by sailors suffering from scurvy. By the wood, primroses and wood sorrel decorate the route. Among woodland birds is the wood warbler, a summer visitor to deciduous woodlands and, in Yorkshire, almost entirely confined to woods on the valley slopes, especially where there are beech trees. It is a handsome bird, with yellow-green upper parts and a yellow breast; listen for its high-pitched trill. Where the path enters the wood, turn up

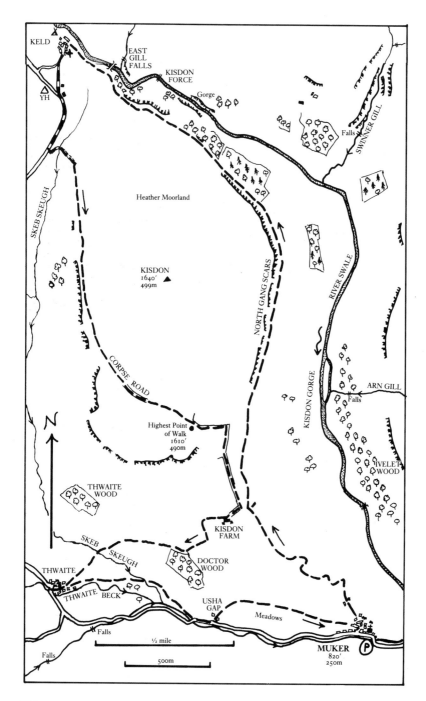

KELD

EAST
GILL
FALLS

KISDON
FORCE

Gorge

SWINNER GILL

Falls

YH

SKEB SKEUGH

Heather Moorland

NORTH GANG SCARS

RIVER SWALE

KISDON
1640'
499m

CORPSE ROAD

KISDON GORGE

ARN GILL

Falls

Highest Point
of Walk
1610'
490m

N

IVELET
WOOD

THWAITE
WOOD

KISDON
FARM

SKEB

SKEUGH

DOCTOR
WOOD

THWAITE

THWAITE BECK

USHA
GAP

Meadows

Falls

½ mile

Falls

500m

MUKER
820'
250m

P

Muker and Kisdon Hill.

along the low, broken wall, then descend below a limestone scar to the sign for Kisdon Force and a chance to view this attractive double waterfall. Take care along the narrow path, which can be slippery where it drops steeply to the falls. The Swale tumbles thirty feet (9m) here into a shady ravine with steep walls of rock on both sides, spectacular after a good downpour. Harry Speight described the gorge as having 'one of the grandest combinations of rock and water scenery in the country'.

Return to the path and, 200 yards (180m) further on, go down to the footbridge to see the pretty East Gill Falls where the tributary stream descends over a triple staircase. Retreat once again to the main path which leads into Keld.

This is the last village along the road up Swaledale. Situated 1,050 feet (320m) above sea level, it nestles comfortably in a hollow away from the road. The fine, well-built sandstone cottages surround a small square, originally the green. It has been said that Keld has more public buildings than many a place ten times its size, including the village hall and reading room, literary institute, United Reform chapel, library and public toilets. The inn, school and post office are now closed.

Among the tough inhabitants who have lived here was one Edward Stillman, appointed in 1789 as independent pastor when the chapel was in ruins. To raise money for it, he walked to London and back, raised £700 as he went, and deducted 6d (2½p) for his own expenses. The new chapel was built and he stayed on for forty-eight years. The chapel, now the United Reform Church, was rebuilt again in 1860, complete with bell and sundial. At the turn of the century, Neddy Nick (Richard Alderson) became well known for his 'rock band', musical stones which he had gathered from the riverbed. He used to play them and sing along, to the entertainment of local people. Susan Peacock, the proprietress and outstanding personality of the Tan Hill Inn for thirty-five years, was buried in the graveyard in 1937 when forty cars joined the cortège from Tan Hill to Keld.

At the head of the dale, Keld is an ideal centre for walkers. The wilderness of moor and fell stretch out in all directions, while near at hand are the side valleys of Stonesdale, Whitsundale, Birkdale and Swinner Gill, and in the river gorge itself are half a dozen exciting waterfalls. This is the crossroads of two long-distance footpaths, the Pennine Way and the Coast-to-Coast path, and is the halfway stage of the latter route from St Bees Head to Robin Hood's Bay. The Youth Hostel on the main road at Keld Green and the riverside campsite have regular visitors through the year. Park Lodge Farm sells ice cream, milk and soft drinks.

Walk up the village and fork left to the main road, and left again. The house at the petrol station was formerly the Cat Hole Inn, a commanding position on the main road for passing travellers. A quarter of a mile (400m) further on, turn left onto the Corpse Road. The track immediately crosses the little stream of Skeb Skeugh ('sheep wood'), all that remains to drain this huge valley. In fact the Swale took this route in pre-glacial times. Then, towards the end of the Ice Age, the way was plugged by glacial debris which forced the surging waters of melting glaciers to find another route, and the present valley on the east side of Kisdon was created.

Climb steeply up and consider the pallbearers who, before 1580, set off along here on the twelve mile (19km) two day trek to the nearest burial ground at Grinton Church. The coffin was carried in a wicker basket and relief bearers took over at

villages on the route. Kisdon comes from the Celtic meaning 'small detatched hill', a perfect description for this island of moorland where there is a resident grouse community and where lapwing, skylark, curlew and golden plover are all breeding birds. The Buttertubs road comes into view now, with Lovely Seat beyond it and High Seat and High Nab Hill to the right.

Across the valley of Skeb Skeugh lies Angram, a small hamlet of a few scattered cottages and farms, clustered on the top of the hill. Angram has the honour of being the highest village in Swaledale at 1,190 feet (362m) above sea level, 140 feet (42m) higher than Keld. In Victorian times, the larger population was thirsty for knowledge, for Angram had not only a school for boys, Mrs Cope's school for girls but also an evening school for adults.

Pass over the shoulder of Kisdon, here 100 feet (30m) below the highest point which lies 1,635 feet (500m) above sea level, and look down on the Swale and the splendid view of Muker in the valley below, with Swaledale stretching into the distance to the east.

Join a walled lane and descend to the Pennine Way (near to the route of the early part of the walk where a quick return to Muker is possible). Turn right into a walled lane and pass Kisdon Farm, following the Pennine Way signs to Thwaite. The path becomes a grassy bank as it traverses the south-facing slopes of Kisdon. At first, on limestone, the flowers include wild thyme, mouse-eared hawkweed, and birdsfoot trefoil. The view below is of Usha Gap, where a landslip has narrowed the valley and where Straw Beck runs towards Muker.

The vegetation changes to ling, bilberry, bracken and tormentil – indicating an acid soil – and the path passes Doctor Wood, a rare birch wood. Look amongst the heather for cow-wheat which makes its appearance

Muker, with its literary institute and bridge.

in a botanically interesting situation. In the Dales it is a rare species occurring in dry heathland, where its presence is a reminder that the area was once wooded. Like its cousin yellow rattle, cow-wheat attatches itself to grass roots to extract minerals; it has pairs of yellow tubular flowers.

Cross the beck by the stone bridge and, a field or two later, enter Thwaite. The village lies near the road junction which leads to Hawes over the Buttertubs Pass, the Buttertubs being impressive limestone potholes on both sides of the road. In 1899 the beck, which drains the side of Shunner Fell down Stockdale, brought disaster to Thwaite when floods damaged many houses, and sheds, animals and gardens were swept away.

The village was the home of Richard and Cherry Kearton, who became pioneers in wildlife photography. They are remembered for ingenious ways of obtaining close-up photographs. They built a papier-mâché cow in which they hid with camera equipment and moved forward towards their targets; and to get near a high nest, they tied the tripod to long poles and Richard climbed on his brother's shoulders to take the photograph. Today a stone lintel, delightfully carved with a line of birds and animals, marks the cottage where they lived. Named after the famous pair is the Kearton guesthouse and restaurant, where good home cooking is available.

From Thwaite, return, to begin with, along the same path, then keep to the right along the beckside, signed 'Muker'. There are some interesting barns of varying sizes and styles, and by early July the upright and proud melancholy thistles are in bloom in the meadows. Cross a stone bridge on the way and come out onto the road at Usha Gap Bridge. Turn left along the road for 100 yards (90m) or so, past the campsite and left via Usha Gap Farm through the fields to Muker. The nearby Duckingtub Bridge marks a place on the beck where sheep dipping was traditionally carried out.

WALK 19: KELD TO TAN HILL

Start: Keld. Grid Ref: 893 012
Distance: 10½ miles (17km)
OS Maps: Outdoor Leisure 30 or Landranger 91
Walking Time: 5 hours

After a scenic walk along Cotterby Scar and Whitsundale to Ravenseat, there follows a magnificent traverse of the open fell in the lee of Robert's Seat to reach the Tan Hill Inn. After refreshment at England's highest pub, return south on the Pennine Way, along the edge of West Stonesdale, back to Keld. The main interests are the outstanding views, the historic coal industry of Tan Hill and the inn. The Pennine Way section is boggy, so is best after a dry period or a sharp frost. There is a new car park at Park Lodge Farm in Keld village.

The little hamlet of Keld is peaceful enough today, but has not always been so. Before the dissolution of the monasteries there was a chapel here, mentioned by Leland in 1530, which had to be closed after a riot of the local people. Edmund Cooper mentions some verses, written 300 years later by a local farmer, that describe a fight in Keld Chapel which might well have been the same affray. They tell of a stranger who stood up during a service and asked if anyone knew of a calf he could buy. The people considered this a blasphemous use of their chapel and told the man to be gone. When he refused, a fight broke out which left the church so badly damaged that it was never re-consecrated and became disused. The next mention of the chapel came in 1695 when one shilling was spent 'for walling up Keld Chapel door'. Muker Church was built in 1580, but Keld waited until 1789 for Edward Stillman and his new chapel.

Walk up out of the village and take the right fork to the main road. The large building on the left is the youth hostel, once a hunting lodge, and near the road junction is the Methodist chapel, built in 1841.

Turn along the road to the right for 760 yards (700m) to the Tan Hill road end, the bus terminus for the twice-weekly service from Richmond. The road sign says 'Tan Hill 3¾'. Cross the single stone arch of Park Bridge, where you have a fine view upstream of Wain Wath Force backed by the white limestone cliffs of Cotterby Scar.

At the first bend in the road, take the footpath left signed 'Raven Seat 2' which leads along the top of the high and impressive cliff of Cotterby Scar. Through the birches and yews, look out for another view of Wain Wath Force and, further along, of the smelt mill for Lane End Mines, now used as a farm store. Several streams have made notches in the scar limestone, which provide arresting glimpses to the river below and which, after heavy rain, make a series of waterfalls. Built on solid rock, the stone arch of Low Bridge comes into view and on the near bank is a limekiln.

Keep up past a small farm, then the abandoned farmhouse of Smithy Holme. It was here that the verses about the Keld riot were discovered among some old papers, left by Anthony Clarkson, who lived here and who died in 1847.

Whitsundale is a quiet side valley, this part of which is known as Red Gulch Gill. It is deep and scenic with some interesting features. At Oven Mouth, the river has created a precipitous cliff and far below is an isolated table of rock, around which the

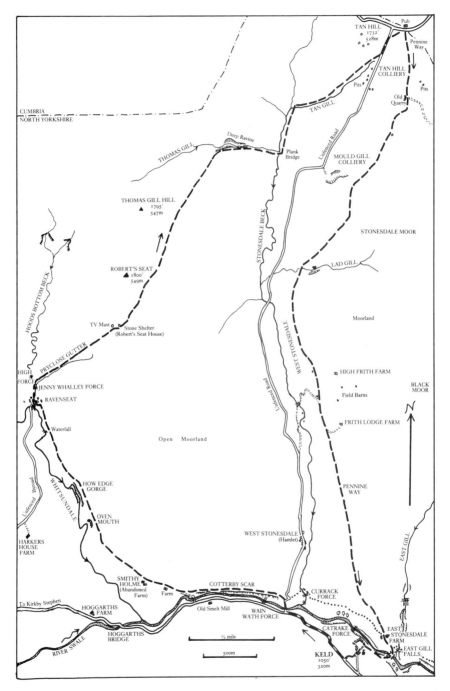

TAN HILL
1732'
528m

Pub

Pennine
Way

TAN HILL
COLLIERY

Pits

Old
Quarry

Pits

CUMBRIA
NORTH YORKSHIRE

THOMAS GILL

Deep Ravine

Plank
Bridge

TAN GILL

Unfenced Road

MOULD GILL
COLLIERY

STONESDALE BECK

STONESDALE MOOR

THOMAS GILL HILL
1795'
547m

ROBERT'S SEAT
1800'
549m

LAD GILL

Moorland

HOODS BOTTOM BECK

PRYCLOSE GUTTER

TV Mast
Stone Shelter
(Robert's Seat House)

HIGH
FORCE

JENNY WHALLEY FORCE

RAVENSEAT

Waterfall

WEST STONESDALE

Unfenced Road

HIGH FRITH FARM

Field Barns

FRITH LODGE FARM

BLACK
MOOR

N

Open   Moorland

PENNINE
WAY

Unfenced Byroad

WHITSUNDALE

HOW EDGE
GORGE

OVEN
MOUTH

HARKERS
HOUSE
FARM

WEST STONESDALE
(Hamlet)

EAST GILL

SMITHY
HOLME
(Abandoned
Farm)

Farm

COTTERBY SCAR

CURRACK
FORCE

To Kirkby Stephen

HOGGARTHS
FARM

Old Smelt Mill

WAIN
WATH FORCE

CATRAKE
FORCE

EAST
STONESDALE
FARM

HOGGARTHS
BRIDGE

RIVER SWALE

¼ mile

500m

KELD
1050'
320m

EAST GILL
FALLS

115

river makes a deep curve. Further on, the sandstone cliffs come close together in How Edge Gorge. The gorge is worth a visit if you have not already seen it. Otherwise, to avoid going down and up again, keep to the high-level path and pass by two or three field barns until, suddenly, Ravenseat is seen close ahead, with a waterfall in the foreground to complete the picturesque view.

Go through the gate, and left through a second, to cross the beck over a plank bridge. Ravenseat is now a working sheep farm and a cottage, though 150 years ago it housed eleven families. The men worked in the coalmines and made the daily trek to Tan Hill and back in all kinds of weather. In winter they journeyed twice a day in the dark and never saw daylight until Sunday. The packhorse bridge has survived rebuilding or widening because modern traffic uses the ford alongside it. One of the barns has a small rounded window and is said to have been a chapel of the Inghamite sect.

Go up through the farmyard alongside a stream, where the little waterfall of Jenny Whalley Force pours into a dark hollow. A little further upstream is the miniature cascade of High Force.

Common sandpipers are to be seen by the becks at Ravenseat, but look out too for the unobtrusive dunlin, slightly smaller, which in breeding plumage has a black belly patch, and chestnut and grey back. Dunlin are not uncommon but widely scattered on the moors. The brief trill of the displaying cock bird is an enchanting sound on a still evening in spring.

The route is across the stream, between the two waterfalls, and up the side of Pryclose Gutter. This is the path taken not only by the miners from Ravenseat but by packhorse teams from Tan Hill, carrying coals over into Mallerstangdale, to Lady Anne's castle at Pendragon and Lord

Wharton's estate at Wharton Hall. In 1670, Philip Lord Wharton who owned the Tan Hill coal mines had an agreement for 150 free loads to be delivered to his residence at Wharton Hall. The route was over the packhorse bridge at Ravenseat and along Ney Gill to Birkdale and the road to Kirkby Stephen. This is now a section of Coast-to-Coast path.

From Pryclose Gutter, pass a TV aerial on the left and head for a square structure on the horizon. The sturdy, high-walled building provides welcome shelter for walkers, but it is marked on old OS maps as Robert's Seat House. In the days when poaching was common, it was a simple gamekeeper's bothy and, on one occasion near here, desperate poachers shot a gamekeeper below the knee, telling him he would be shot higher up if he moved!

The views from the shelter are panoramic. Kisdon looms large in the near distance with Rogan's Seat, Lovely Seat and Great Shunner Fell in the background. But to the north is the first view of the Tan Hill Inn, two and a half miles (4km) away and beckoning you on.

The path is a worn green line through the springy turf of the open fell, but not difficult to follow. (In poor visibility, take a bearing of 30° from north for the next mile (1,600m) or so, to Thomas Gill, keeping to the same level.) This stretch makes excellent walking. The way is sheltered from westerly winds by the ridge of Robert's Seat and Thomas Gill Hill, while on the right are a series of peat hags. There is an immense skyline to watch, the distant Pennine horizons ahead, the stone men of Nine Standards coming into view on the left and Water Crag and Rogan's Seat on the right. On a beautiful, clear spring day, at 1,700 feet (520m) above sea level on this ancient packhorse route, there is no better fell walking in the Dales.

Avoiding any descent to the right, the

lightly-worn path comes to the deep, black shale gully of Thomas Gill. Turn down alongside the gill to the wooden hut and plank bridge over Stonesdale Beck. Follow the beck upstream on the right bank, past a small waterfall and sheepfold to a tributary stream on the right, marked by a small sandstone bluff. This is Tan Gill which, by following the left side, leads you to the road and to the Tan Hill Inn.

Tan is Celtic meaning fire, so perhaps the discovery and use of coal here goes back 2,000 years or more. The first record is of a pit having a profit of one shilling in 1296 and the last mine to close was in the 1930s, so between these times there has been a long history of coalmining. In 1384, the Takkan Tan Mine was supplying coal to Richmond Castle and, during the lead-mining period, the smelt mills had an insatiable appetite for this valuable commodity. Tan Hill Colliery is south of the inn, an area of deep shafts near the road, and Mould Gill Colliery is to the south of this. King's Pit and William Gill collieries lie to the east and supplied Wharton's smelt mills in the seventeenth century and, later, Old Gang smelt mill. A hundred years ago it was a common sight to see dozens of carts arriving here in the early morning to take coal for winter fires.

England's highest pub lies 1,732 feet (528m) above sea level. It has an attraction which extends far beyond the Yorkshire Dales and, recently, new accommodation has been added to serve the large number of visitors who call in or who wish to stay the night. There is always a cheerful welcome and a fire burns continuously in the bar. Coffee, hot food and Theakston's ale are readily available to weary Pennine Way walkers who stagger in here and all other visitors who cannot resist this remote and historic place. The sheep fair takes place here in May, and is *the* show for Swaledale sheep. Prize-winning rams command

The Tan Hill Inn was built in 1737, and was once known as the Kings Pit after a nearby coalmine.

prices of up to £30,000 at auctions held later in the season. Susan Peacock was the proprietress and outstanding personality of Tan Hill Inn from 1902 to 1937 and at her funeral, forty cars joined the cortège from Tan Hill to Keld.

Before leaving Tan Hill, have a look at the view of Stainmore from the rear of the inn, stretching away to Barnard Castle and Teesdale where white farmhouses dot the landscape. There is also a plaque in memory of Susan Peacock.

The return is made along the track opposite the front door of the pub, signed 'Pennine Way'. Fork right near an old quarry, after which the route is marked by cairns. Remains of the coalmines are surprisingly few and have to be searched out, the moor having taken over once more. It can be wet and boggy on the way down, but there is a fine prospect of West Stonesdale and, to the north, the distant hills include Cross Fell, the highest point in the Pennines at 2,929 feet (893m), and Great

East Gill Falls near Keld.

Dun Fell with its prominent white radar/ weather station on the top. Mickle Fell, to the right again, is an army danger zone and you may well hear the distant boom of firing from that direction.

Descend to Lad Gill, where steep banks of black shale add a point of interest to the bleak moorland. Then, suddenly, half a dozen fine barns and the two farmhouses of High Frith and Frith Lodge appear ahead. How the farmers managed to produce enough hay to fill all those barns gives some idea of the tireless work involved and the constant battle against the moor, ever ready to take over.

The meadows of West Stonesdale are noted for the variety of wild flowers, but look out around here for the black grouse (or blackcock). Bigger and plumper than the red grouse, the black grouse is distin-guished by its glossy blue-black colour, longer neck, lyre-shaped tail and white wing-bar. The female is smaller and grey-brown. They often congregate on wall tops or in birch trees. At dawn at the end of winter, these fascinating birds display in a *lek* or courtship area. There can be twenty cocks, each with fanned tail held erect, jousting in a mock battle with a rival male to win a hen.

The peaceful hamlet of West Stonesdale is seen on the right, ahead is the flat top of Lovely Seat and Kisdon stands out with its crowning cairn. Descend to East Stonesdale Farm and the new footbridge over the Swale. A view of the pretty East Gill Falls is a final bonus to this lovely walk, before crossing the bridge and returning to Keld up the far bank.

WALK 20: NINE STANDARDS RIGG

Start: Car park at Hollow Mill Cross. Grid Ref: 812 040
Distance: 7 miles (11km)
OS Maps: Pathfinder 608 or Landranger 92
Walking Time: 3½ hours

On the very borders of Swaledale, Yorkshire and the Dales National Park, this exhilarating walk (hardly a climb) starts at the scene of a seventeenth century murder, crosses a high-level limestone pavement and rises less than 500 feet (150m) to the summit of Nine Standards Rigg at 2,173 feet (662m) above sea level. The nine stone towers overlook Mallerstangdale and the upper Eden, with panoramic views to the Lake District mountains. A gentle descent along the moor leads into Birkdale and the road back to Hollow Mill Cross. It is a wild area with little or no shelter. There is a car park at Hollow Mill Cross, which lies on the B6270 between Keld and Kirkby Stephen.

Hollow Mill Cross once stood here, by the road from Swaledale to Kirkby Stephen, at the county boundary between Yorkshire and Westmorland (now Cumbria). The cross was very old and marked on sixteenth century maps. However, it has long since vanished, but the name remains, as does the tale of a terrible murder that has been told and retold by generations of local dalesfolk.

On the 24th March in the year 1664, a stocking buyer called John Smith, having slept the night at James Alderson's farm in Keld, set out up Birkdale on his way over into Westmorland. When he got to Hollow Mill Cross he was brutally murderered and robbed. The murderer was never caught, but a certain Westmorland miner named Hutchinson was under strong suspicion. This man, presumably because of his guilt, had hallucinations and heard voices in the night, so he tried to put the blame onto James Alderson and his two sons. Two and a half years after the murder, the case was heard in York, but Hutchinson's story was so full of holes that the jury dismissed it. A petition, extolling the honesty and virtue of James Alderson, was presented, having been signed by 106 Swaledale men.

At Hollow Mill Cross there still stand two boundary stones, one for each county. They read: 'The Township of Nateby 1856' and 'Hamlet of Birkdale, County of York'. The boundary is well-chosen, for here is the watershed of England between the drainage of the Swale, which goes into the North Sea, and that of the Eden which flows into the Irish Sea. It is the roof of the Pennines and it is also the edge of the Yorkshire Dales National Park.

From the boundary car park, walk up the road for a quarter of a mile (400m) and turn right by some large stones at the roadside, onto a track through the limestone outcrops of Tailbrigg (Tailbridge on the map). It is less than half a mile (650m) to the highest point on the road at the head of the pass where, on a clear day, there is a fine view over the Eden Valley and beyond. It is here that the hang-gliders and para-gliders test their skills and find thermals which rise against the steep Tailbrigg escarpment.

The limestone plateau which the path traverses contains, for Swaledale, a rare exposure of limestone pavements, and the flora is unusual. It is a Site of Special Scientific Interest which extends southward on both sides of the park boundary.

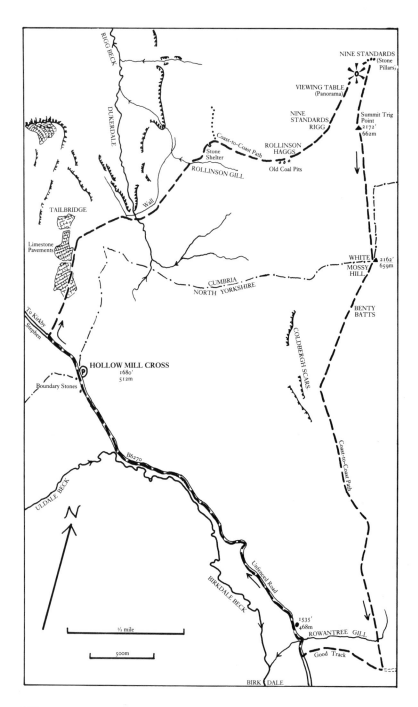

RIGG BECK

NINE STANDARDS
(Stone Pillars)

VIEWING TABLE
(Panorama)

DUKERDALE

NINE
STANDARDS
RIGG

Summit Trig
Point
▲ 2172'
662m

Coast-to-Coast Path

ROLLINSON
HAGGS

Stone
Shelter

ROLLINSON GILL

Old Coal Pits

Wall

TAILBRIDGE

Limestone
Pavements

WHITE
MOSSY
HILL

2162'
659m

CUMBRIA
NORTH YORKSHIRE

BENTY
BATTS

To Kirkby
Stephen

COLDBERGH SCARS

HOLLOW MILL CROSS
1680'
512m

P

Boundary Stones

Coast-to-Coast Path

B6270

ULDALE BECK

N

BIRKDALE BECK

Unfenced Road

1535'
468m

ROWANTREE GILL

½ mile

500m

Good Track

BIRKDALE

The glaciated valley of Dukerdale.

Soils are very thin and plant roots are more or less in contact with bedrock. Blue moorgrass, rare in other parts of the country, grows well and is accompanied by rockrose, spring whitlow-grass, mountain pansy and fairy flax. The plant with the fine name of spring whitlow-grass (or common whitlow-grass) is not a grass but a tiny white-flowered annual with a basal rosette of leaves, which in rocky places may be little more than an inch (2½cm) high. Two other flowers which you will be lucky to find are mossy saxifrage and mountain everlasting, also typical of this upland limestone grassland.

Pass a series of potholes and, on the right, a small tarn. There are gritstone boulders perched on the limestone pavement, placed there by the last ice sheet and, as they don't match the underlying rock,

are termed erratics. Wheatears, lapwings and larks keep you company and, approaching the corner of a wall, the path curves round to the right to give a view left of the spectacular gorge of Dukerdale, ringed by high rocky scars.

Cross Rigg Beck and climb up the hillside with a wall on the left. Rigg Beck can be seen far below as it meanders along the glacial bowl of Dukerdale. Turn away from the wall (to the right) and head for the 'cairn' on the horizon. The path is quite clear and the cairn turns out to be a substantial stone shelter on a high shoulder, from where there are extensive views of Great Shunner Fell, Wild Boar Fell and the Howgills.

Bear slightly to the right and, after 100 yards (90m) or so, join the Coast-to-Coast footpath which comes in from the left up

The mysterious stone towers on the summit of Nine Standards Rigg.

the north side of Dukerdale. The route takes you past some old coal pits and peat hags, named Rollinson Haggs on the map, and gently climbs to the trig point which marks the summit of Nine Standards Rigg. From here, carry on to the viewpoint and the stone towers. The viewing table with its metal plate was erected by members of the Kirkby Stephen Fell Search Team to commemorate the wedding of Prince Charles and Lady Diana in 1981. On a clear day the panorama is breathtaking: the Howgills, the Lake District mountains, the scarp edge of the northern Pennines with Cross Fell and a bird's-eye view of the Eden Valley; Mallerstang Edge and Wild Boar Fell are nearer landmarks.

Standing out dramatically on the skyline are the Nine Standards – stone towers, mostly round and neatly built out of flagstone from the summit rock, which line up on the northern shoulder of the mountain, overlooking the Vale of Eden. There are many guesses as to their origin. The local name of 'stone men' may have led to the suggestion that they were built to scare marauding Scots into thinking that English soldiers were on guard here. Bill Mitchell reckons the figure nine is an important element and that they could be connected to St Ninian, who may have converted heathens to Christianity in Mallerstang. St Ninian's Church at Broughham, near Penrith, is known as Ninekirks. While at

Nine Standards, keep a lookout for ravens which haunt the crags, often in pairs, their deep, dry voices, large size and acrobatic flight helping to identify them.

Return to the trig point which, at 2,172 feet (662m), is the highest point of the fell. Descend about half a mile (1km) along the ridge (to the south-south-west) to the top of White Moss, then over Benty Batts, to a wind shelter and stone tower. From the ridge, Birkdale Tarn and the whole of Swaledale can be seen ahead. The hilltop tarn was made to provide water for Lane End leadmines, and is now a breeding place for a colony of black-headed gulls. It also provided a fine silver sand which, when mixed with tar or beef fat and smeared onto a strip of wood, made a 'strickle' to sharpen scythes. After two and a half miles (4km) from the summit the path comes out onto a vehicle track, an ancient route from Tan Hill to Kirkby Stephen and here improved for grouse shooting parties. Turn right to join the Kirkby Stephen road near Rowantree Gill.

This is Birkdale, locally called Birtle. It is a lonely and bleak place. The Scots, and raiders from Stainmore known as 'Moss Troopers', came over into Birkdale from time to time, wreaking havoc. Stone House, lower down the dale, is the traditional site of a battle with the Scots in 1347, when Ellerton Priory was raided.

Centuries later a gang of poaching miners, known as 'Weardale Warriors', used to come over, instilling fear into local farmers. On one occasion about 1830, the gang, under the leadership of strong man, Paul Armstrong, was observed by the gamekeeper Cherry Kearton to enter a cowhouse at Crook Seal Farm, where they settled for the night. (It is now a ruin, half a mile (800m) down the road towards Keld from Rowantree Gill.) The gamekeeper assembled a group of six other local farmers, each with a shotgun, who surrounded the cowhouse and waited for dawn. On seeing Armstrong come to the door, the Swaledalers jumped up, guns at the ready. A shot was fired, the leader, who tried to rush them, was knocked on the head, the gang surrendered and were marched off.

Half an hour's trudge up the unfenced road brings you back to the car park at Hollow Mill Cross.

SELECTED READING

General:
Ron and Marlene Freethy, *Discovering the Yorkshire Dales* (Donald, 1991). A readable guide to the Dales, especially history but also some natural history.
Marie Hartley and Joan Ingilby, *The Yorkshire Dales* (Dent, 1956; reprinted Smith Settle, 1991). A compact description of all the dales.
Richard Muir, *The Dales of Yorkshire – A Portrait* (Macmillan, 1991). Readable and authoritative.
Tony Waltham, *Yorkshire Dales National Park* (Webb and Bower, 1987). The latest official guide to the National Park. Well-written and informative.
Geoffrey N Wright, *The Yorkshire Dales* (David and Charles, 1986). Informative on natural history, history, mining and quarrying. Includes a gazetteer.

Geology:
Derek Brumhead, *Geology Explained in the Yorkshire Dales and on the Yorkshire Coast* (David and Charles, 1979). Contains leadmine itineraries.
Arthur Raistrick and John L Illingworth, *The Face of North West Yorkshire* (Dalesman, 1959). A background to geology and natural vegetation.
K C Dunham and A A Wilson, *Geology of the Northern Pennine Orefield, Vol 2* (British Geological Survey, 1985). Very detailed Dales geology.

History:
Edmund Bogg, *The Wild Borderland of Richmondshire* and *Regal Richmond and the Land of the Swale* (Elliot Stock, 1909).
Edmund Cooper, *History of Swaledale* (Dalesman, 1973).
Edmund Cooper, *Muker, the Story of a Yorkshire Parish* (Dalesman, 1948).
R Fieldhouse and B Jennings, *A history of Richmond and Swaledale* (Phillimore, 1978). The standard text containing much original research.
Marie Hartley and Joan Ingilby, *The Old Hand-knitters of the Dales* (Dent, 1951; fourth edition Dalesman, 1988).
R W Morris, *Yorkshire through Place Names* (David and Charles, 1982). Relates settlement and place names to the geography and geology.
Ella Pontefract and Marie Hartley, *Swaledale* (Dent, 1934; reprinted Smith Settle, 1988). Delightful personal stories of the dale.
Arthur Raistrick, *Pennine Walls* (Dalesman, 1988). Who built them, why and how.
Harry Speight, *Romantic Richmondshire* (Elliot Stock, 1897). A reliable history of Swaledale and Wensleydale.
Sandra K Wood, *Swaledale – The Spirit Speaks Loud* (Corporate Link, 1989). Five volumes (planned) of interesting old photographs of Swaledale with notes of individuals, families and houses.
Geoffrey N Wright, *Roads and Trackways of the Yorkshire Dales* (Moorland Publishing, 1985). An attractive study of a little recorded subject.

Leadmining:
John Hardy, *The Hidden Side of Swaledale* (Frank Peters, 1990). Large, colourful and enthusiastic.
Brian Lee (ed), *Lead Mining in Swaledale* (Faust Publications, 1985). Personal reminiscences from a manuscript of E R Fawcett.
David Morris, *The Dalesmen of the Mississippi River* (Sessions, 1989). The story of families who left Swaledale for a new life in a leadmining area of the upper Mississippi.
Arthur Raistrick, *The Lead Industry of Wensleydale and Swaledale* (2 volumes, Moorland Publishing, 1975). A standard work.

Natural History:
Sylvia Arnold, *Wild Flowers of the Yorkshire Dales* (Hutton, 1988).
M J Delany (ed), *Yorkshire Mammals* (University of Bradford, 1985). Detailed description of species with useful distribution maps.
Alan Drewitt (compiled by), *The Vegetation of the Yorkshire Dales National Park* (YDNP, 1991). Very useful on plants and their habitats.
J Ferguson-Lees (*et al*), *The Shell Guide to the Birds of Britain and Ireland* (Michael Joseph, 1983). One of the best general bird books.
W R Mitchell and R W Robson, *Pennine Birds* (Dalesman, 1973). Useful for birds of the uplands.
Franklyn Perring, *RSNC Guide to British Wild Flowers* (Country Life Books, 1984). Very useful for learning common species and sorting out 'look-alikes'.
Roger S Smith, *Conservation of Northern Upland Meadows* (YDNP, 1985).

Walking:
Arthur Gemmell, *Upper Swaledale Footpath Map and Guide* (Stile Publications, 1986). Beautifully drawn and annotated map.
Mike Harding, *Walking the Dales* (Michael Joseph, 1986). Includes two walks in Swaledale.
Colin Speakman, *Walking in the Yorkshire Dales* (Hale, 1982). A comprehensive and authoritative guide.
A Wainwright, *A Coast to Coast Walk* (Westmorland Gazette, 1972). Includes the length of Swaledale.

Fiction:
Thomas Armstrong, *Adam Brunskill* (Collins, 1952). Authentic background to a story of nineteenth century leadmining in Swaledale.
H F M Prescott, *The Man on a Donkey* (Eyre & Spottiswoode, 1952). A story centred round Marrick Priory in the 1530s at the time of the Dissolution and the Pilgrimage of Grace.

INDEX

128